Renew

- By Knit Picks -

Photography by Amy Setter

Printed in the United States of America

First Printing, 2018

ISBN 978-1-62767-191-0

Versa Press, Inc
800-447-7829

www.versapress.com

CONTENTS

CATARAQUI CREEK

by Nicole Tavares

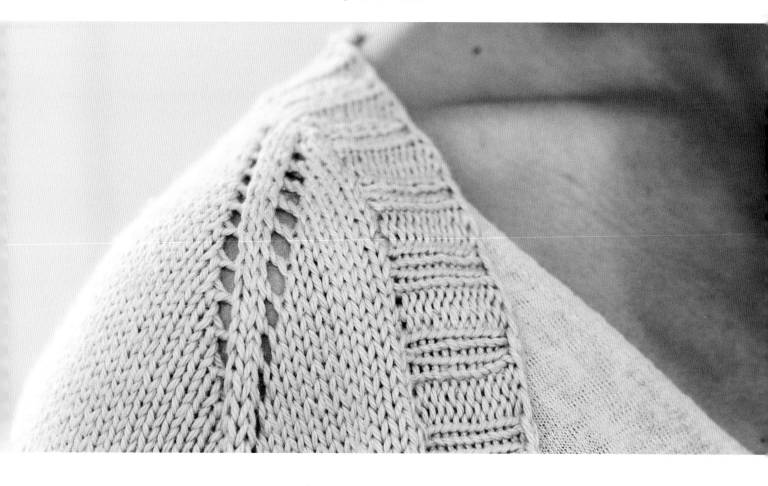

FINISHED MEASUREMENTS

34.25 (39, 42, 46.5, 49.75, 53.75, 57.75, 62, 65.5)" actual finished bust measurement with open front; to fit 30-34 (34-38, 38-42, 42-46, 46-50, 50-54, 54-58, 58-62, 62-66)" bust.

YARN

Knit Picks Comfy Sport
(75% Pima Cotton, 25% Acrylic; 136 yards/50g): Sea Foam 24431, 7 (8, 9, 10, 12, 13, 15, 15, 16) balls

NEEDLES

US 4 (3.5mm) 32" or longer circular needles, or one size smaller than size to obtain gauge
US 5 (3.75mm) 32" or longer circular needles, and optionally DPNs or two 24" circular needles for two circular technique, or size to obtain gauge

NOTIONS

Yarn Needle
Stitch Markers
Scrap yarn or stitch holder

GAUGE

22 sts and 28 rows = 4" in St st on larger needles, blocked

For pattern support, contact
nicole.tavares.151@gmail.com

Notes:

Cataraqui Creek is a seamless top-down cardigan with raglan sleeves and a narrow shawl collar. This sweater is designed to be worn open and features delicate lace details on the bottom hem and the sleeves. The lace pattern is presented in both charted and written form.

When working flat, read the charts RS rows (odd numbers) from right to left, and WS rows (even numbers) from left to right. When working in the rnd, read all chart rows as RS rows, from right to left.

Rib & Eyelet Stitch (worked flat over a multiple of 6 plus 2 sts)
Row 1 (RS): K2, (P1, YO, K2tog TBL, P1, K2) to end.
Row 2 (WS): P2, (K1, P2) to end.
Row 3: K2, (P1, K2tog, YO, P1, K2) to end.
Row 4: Rep Row 2.
Rep Rows 1-4 for pattern.

Rib & Eyelet Stitch (worked in the round over a multiple of 6 stitches)
Rnd 1: (P1, YO, K2tog TBL, P1, K2) to end.
Rnd 2: (P1, K2) to end.
Rnd 3: (P1, K2tog, YO, P1, K2) to end.
Rnd 4: Rep Rnd 2.
Rep Rnds 1-4 for pattern.

Stockinette Stich (worked flat)
Row 1(RS): K to end.
Row 2 (WS): P to end.
Rep Rows 1-2 for pattern.

Stockinette Stich (worked in the round)
All Rnds: K to end.

DIRECTIONS

Body
CO 56 (76, 84. 100, 120, 138, 146, 146, 154) sts using the Long-Tail CO.
Set-up Row (WS): P2 for Right Front, PM, P4 (9, 10, 14, 21, 26, 28, 24, 25) for Right Sleeve, PM, P44 (54, 60, 68, 74, 82, 86, 94, 100) for Back, PM, P4 (9, 10, 14, 21, 26, 28, 24, 25) for Left Sleeve, PM, P2 for Left Front.

Raglan Increase Rows
Row 1 (RS) : *K to 1 st before M, YO, K1, SM, K1, YO; rep from * three times, K to end. 8 sts inc.
Row 2 (WS): P to end.

Work Raglan Increase Rows a total of 25 (26, 28, 30, 32, 34, 37, 39, 41) times. 27 (28, 30, 32, 34, 36, 39, 41, 43) Left Front and Right Front sts, 54 (61, 66, 74, 85, 94, 102, 102, 107) sts each Sleeve, 94 (106, 116, 128, 138, 150, 160, 172, 182) Back sts. 256 (284, 308, 340, 376, 410, 442, 458, 482) total sts.

Separation Row: K27 (28, 30, 32, 34, 36, 39, 41, 43) remove M, place next 54 (61, 66, 74, 85, 94, 102, 102, 107) sts on a holder, remove M, CO 1 (2, 2, 2, 3, 3, 4, 4, 4) sts using Backwards Loop CO, PM, CO 1 (2, 2, 2, 3, 3, 4, 4, 4) sts using Backwards Loop CO, K94 (106, 116, 128, 138, 150, 160, 172, 182), remove M, place next 54 (61, 66, 74, 85, 94, 102, 102, 107) sts on a holder, rM, CO 1 (2, 2, 2, 3, 3, 4, 4, 4) sts using Backwards Loop CO, PM, CO 1 (2, 2, 2, 3, 3, 4, 4, 4) sts using Backwards Loop CO, K27 (28, 30, 32, 34, 36, 39, 41, 43). 152 (170, 184, 200, 218, 234, 254, 270, 284) sts total.

Next Row (WS): P to end.

Front Panel Increase Rows
Row 1 (RS): K1, M1L, K to 1 st before end, M1R, K1. 2 sts inc.
Row 2 (WS): P to end.

Work Front Panel Increase Rows a total of 2 (3, 3, 5, 2, 4, 4, 3, 5) times. 156 (176, 190, 210, 222, 242, 262, 276, 294) sts total.

Next Row (RS): K to end.
Work 13 (7, 7, 5, 7, 5, 7, 5, 5) rows in St st, beginning with WS row.

Hip Increase Row (RS): *K to 1 before M, M1R, K1, SM, K1, M1L; rep from * once, K to end. 4 sts inc.

Work last 14 (8, 8, 6, 8, 6, 8, 6, 6) rows 5 (9, 8, 10, 10, 12, 11, 13, 13) times total. 176 (212, 222, 250, 262, 290, 306, 328, 346) sts total.

Knit 3 (1, 9, 11, 1, 15, 1, 9, 5) more row(s) in St st, ending with a WS row.

Sizes 42 and 57.75" Only:
Lace Set Up Row (RS): K1, M1L, K to 1 st before end, M1R, K1. 2 sts inc.
Next Row (WS): P to end.

Sizes 46.5, 62, and 65.5" Only:
Lace Set Up Row (RS): *K to 1 before M, M1R, K1, SM, K1, M1L; rep from * once, K to end. 4 sts inc.
Next Row (WS): P to end.

Size 49.75" Only:
Lace Set Up Row (RS): K1, SSK, K to 1 st before end, K2tog, K1. 2 sts dec.
Next Row (WS): P to end.

All Sizes:
Knit in Rib & Eyelet Stitch for 5" or until desired length, ending with Row 4 of the pattern. BO loosely in pattern.

Sleeves
Beginning at the center of the underarm, PU & K1 (2, 2, 2, 3, 3, 4, 4, 4) sts, K54 (61, 66, 74, 85, 94, 102, 102, 107) from st holder, PU & K1 (2, 2, 2, 3, 3, 4, 4, 4) sts from underarm, PM to indicate beginning of rnd. 56 (65, 70, 78, 91, 100, 110, 110, 115) sts total.

Sizes 39, 49.75, and 65.5" Only:
Dec Rnd: K2tog, K to end. - (64, -, -, 90, -, -, -, 114) sts.

All Sizes:
Knit 4 rnds even.
Dec Rnd: K1, K2tog, K to 3 sts before M, SSK, K1. 2 sts dec.

Work these last 5 rnds 1 (5, 5, 9, 12, 17, 22, 22, 24) times total. 54 (54, 60, 60, 66, 66, 66, 66, 66) sts total.

Work in St st. until sleeve measures 17.25 (17.75, 17.75, 18.25, 18.25, 18.75, 19.25, 19.25, 19.25)", or 2.25" before desired length. Switch to smaller needles. Work in Rib and Eyelet Stitch in the rnd for 16 rnds total. BO loosely in pattern.

Repeat for the second sleeve.

Shawl Collar

Using the smaller needles and beginning at the bottom of the Right Front panel, PU & K 2 sts for every 3 rows up the Front Right panel, around the neckline and back down the Front Left panel. Be sure the resulting number of picked up stitches is divisible by 4 plus 2 sts.

Row 1 (WS): P2, (K2, P2) to end.
Row 2 (RS): K2, (P2, K2) to end.

Rep Rows 1-2 2 (3, 3, 4, 5, 5, 5, 7, 7) more times. 7 (9, 9, 11, 13, 13, 13, 17, 17) rows.

Work Row 1 once more. BO loosely in pattern.

Finishing

Weave in ends, wash and block to diagram.

Ribs and Eyelets Flat

	8	7	6	5	4	3	2	1	
4			●			●			
			●	O	/	●			3
2			●			●			
			●	↘	O	●			1

Ribs and Eyelets Circular

6	5	4	3	2	1	
		●			●	4
		●	O	/	●	3
		●			●	2
		●	↘	O	●	1

Legend

□ **knit**
RS: knit stitch
WS: purl stitch

● **purl**
RS: purl stitch
WS: knit stitch

O **yo**
Yarn Over

╱ **k2tog**
Knit two stitches together as one stitch

╲ **k2tog tbl**
Knit two stitches together in back loops as one

□ **Pattern Repeat**

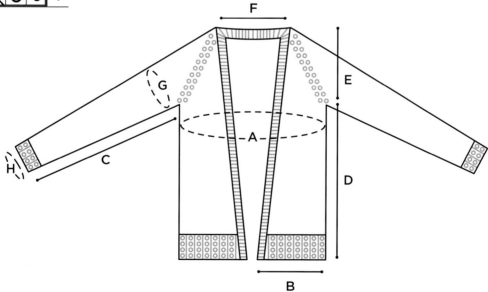

A 30.25 (34, 37.5, 41.5, 44.25, 48, 51.75, 55.25, 58.5)"
B 7.25 (9, 9.5, 10.75, 10.75, 12, 12.75, 13.75, 14.5)"
C 19.5 (20, 20, 20.5, 20.5, 21, 21.5, 21.5, 21.5)"
D 16 (16, 16.5, 17, 17, 18.5, 18.5, 18.5, 18.5)"
E 7.25 (7.5, 8, 8.25, 9.25, 9.75, 10.5, 11.25, 11.75)"
F 8 (9.75, 11, 12.25, 13.5, 15, 15.75, 17, 18.25)"
G 10.25 (11.75, 12.75, 14.25, 16.25, 18.25, 20, 20, 20.75)"
H 9.75 (9.75, 11, 11, 12, 12, 12, 12, 12)"

CLOVERLEAF TOP

by Felecia O'Connell

FINISHED MEASUREMENTS
43.75 (47.5, 51.25, 55, 58.75, 62.5)"
finished bust measurement; garment
is meant to be worn with approx. 8"
positive ease

YARN
Knit Picks CotLin DK
(70% Tanguis Cotton, 30% Linen; 123
yards/50g): Lichen 26674, 5 (6, 6, 7, 7) balls

NEEDLES
US 5 (3.75mm) straight or circular
needles, or size to obtain gauge

NOTIONS
Yarn Needle

GAUGE
17 sts and 24 rows = 4" in Cloverleaf
Stitch pattern, blocked

For pattern support, contact
felecia.o@outlook.com

Notes:

Front and back are worked from the bottom up, as two identical pieces, each beginning with ribbing and ending with an I-cord bind off.

Rib Stitch Pattern
(worked flat over multiples of 8 plus 5 sts)

Row 1 (WS): P1, K1, P1, *K2, P3, K2, P1, rep from * to last 2 sts, K1, P1.

Row 2 (RS): K1, P1, K1, *P2, K3, P2, K1, rep from * to last 2 sts, P1, K1.

Rep Rows 1-2 for pattern.

Cloverleaf Stitch Pattern
(worked flat over multiples of 8 plus 5 sts)

Row 1 (RS): K1, P1, K1, *P2, YO, Sk2p, YO, P2, K1, rep from * to last 2 sts, P1, K1.

Row 2 (WS): P1, K1, P1, *K2, P3, K2, P1, rep from * to last 2 sts, K1, P1.

Row 3: K1, P1, K1, *P2, K1, YO, SSK, P2, K1, rep from * to last 2 sts, P1, K1.

Row 4: Rep Row 2.

Rep Rows 1-4 for pattern.

I-cord Bind-Off
At beginning of row, CO 3 sts using a Knitted or Cable CO.

Step 1: K2, SSK.

Step 2: Place the sts worked back on the LH.

Rep Steps 1 and 2 to end of row.

DIRECTIONS

Front
CO 93 (101, 109, 117, 125, 133) sts.

Work Rib Stitch pattern until piece measures 1.5" from CO edge, ending on a WS row.

Begin Cloverleaf Stitch pattern on next RS row.

Work in Cloverleaf Stitch pattern until piece measures 21.5 (22, 22.5, 23, 23.5, 24)" from CO edge, and ending on Row 4.

Work two rows in St st.

BO using I-cord BO.

Back
Work same as front.

Finishing
Weave in ends, wet block to length and width measurements.

Stitch shoulder and side seams as follows: Place front and back pieces right-sides down on flat surface. Matching I-cord edge to edge, stitch across 5.75 (6.75, 7.75, 8.5, 9.5, 10.25)" on each side for shoulder seams.

With wrong sides facing together, beginning 1.5" from bottom edge, stitch 12.5" side seams, leaving open armholes that measure 8.5 (9, 9.5, 10, 10.5, 11)".

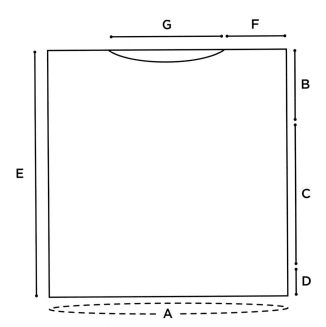

A (Garment Circumference) 43.75 (47.5, 51.25, 55, 58.75, 62.5)"

B (Armhole) 8.5 (9, 9.5, 10, 10.5, 11)"

C (Side Seam) 12.5"

D (Leave Open) 1.5"

E (Garment Length) 22.5 (23, 23.5, 24, 24.5, 25)"

F (Shoulder) 5.75 (6.75, 7.75, 8.5, 9.5, 10.25)"

G (Neck Opening) 10.25 (10.25, 10.25, 10.5, 10.5, 10.75)"

CORRINE TEE

by Cassie Castillo

FINISHED MEASUREMENTS

33 (38, 43, 48, 53, 58)" finished bust measurement; garment is meant to be worn with 1-2" ease.

YARN

Knit Picks Shine Worsted
(60% Pima Cotton, 40% Modal® natural beech wood fiber; 110 yards/50g): Clarity 26680, 9 (11, 13, 14, 16, 18) balls

NEEDLES

US 6 (4 mm) DPNs and 16" circular needles, or two 24" circular needles for two circulars technique, or one 32" or longer needle for Magic Loop technique, or one size smaller than size to obtain gauge
US 7 (4.5 mm) straight or circular needles, or to obtain gauge

NOTIONS

Yarn Needle
Stitch Markers
Scrap yarn or stitch holders

GAUGE

18 sts and 23 rows= 4" in St st on larger needles, blocked
One repeat of Chart A (11 sts and 20 rows) = 2.5" wide and 3" long on larger needles, blocked

Notes:

The Corinne Tee is worked flat in pieces from the bottom up, with short extended cap sleeves. The length measurements in the pattern reflect the blocked length; adjust the length if your blocked and unblocked gauges are different.

Right Lifted Increase (RLI):
Insert right needle front to back into st one row below st on left needle and K.

Left Lifted Increase (LLI):
Insert left needle front to back into st two rows below st on right needle and K.

DIRECTIONS

Front
With larger needles, CO 79 (91, 101, 113, 123, 135) sts.
Sizes 33, 43, 53 Only:
Row 1 (RS): K1, work Chart A to last st, K1.
Row 2 (WS): P1, work Chart A to last st, P1.

Sizes 38, 48, 58 Only:
Row 1 (RS): K1, work Chart C, work Chart A to last 7 sts, work Chart D, K1.
Row 2 (WS): P1, work Chart D, work Chart A to last 7 sts, work Chart C, P1.

All Sizes: Work in established pattern until Rows 1-20 of charts are complete.
Next Row (RS): K33 (39, 44, 50, 55, 61), work Chart B, K to end.
Next Row (WS): P33 (39, 44, 50, 55, 61), work Chart B, P to end.
Dec Row (RS): K1, SSK, work in pattern as established to last 3 sts, K2tog, K1. 2 sts dec.
Rep Dec Row every 6th row 3 more times. 71 (83, 93, 105, 115, 127) sts.

Work in pattern until piece measures 7.25 (7.75, 7.75, 8, 8, 8.25)" from CO edge, ending with a WS row.

Inc Row (RS): K1, RLI, work in pattern to last st, LLI, K1. 2 sts inc.
Rep Inc Row every 14th row 2 more times. 77 (89, 99, 111, 121, 133) sts.

Work in pattern until piece measures 16.25 (16.75, 16.75, 16.75, 16.75, 16.75)" from CO edge, ending with a WS row.

Sleeve Extension:
Working in pattern as established, CO 4 sts at the beginning of the next 2 rows, then 3 sts at the beginning of the next 2 rows, then 2 sts at the beginning of the next 2 rows. 95 (107, 117, 129, 139, 151) sts.

Work in pattern until sleeve opening is 3.75 (4, 4.75, 4.75, 5.75, 6)", ending with a WS row. Body is approximately 21 (21.75, 22.5, 22.5, 23.5, 23.75)".

Divide Neck
Next Row (RS): K41 (47, 52, 58, 63, 69), BO 13 sts, K to end. 41 (47, 52, 58, 63, 69) sts for each front. Place left front sts onto holder.

Right Front
P 1 row. BO 3 (3, 4, 4, 4, 4) sts, then 3 sts, then 2 sts, at the beginning of the next RS rows. P 1 row.

Neck Dec Row (RS): K1, SSK, K to end. 1 st dec.
Rep Neck Dec Row every RS row 1 (2, 3, 4, 4, 5) more times. 31 (36, 39, 44, 49, 54) sts.

Work in pattern until sleeve opening is 5.75 (6.25, 7.25, 7.75, 8.75, 9.25)", ending with a RS row. Body is approximately 23 (24, 25, 25.5, 26.5, 27)". BO 7 (9, 9, 11, 12, 13) sts at the beginning of the next 3 WS rows. BO all sts.

Left Front
Place held left front sts onto needle with WS facing. BO 3 (3, 4, 4, 4, 4) sts, then 3 sts, then 2 sts, at the beginning of the next WS rows.

Neck Dec Row (RS): K to last 3 sts, K2tog, K1. 1 st dec.
Rep Neck Dec Row every RS row 1 (2, 3, 4, 4, 5) more times. 31 (36, 39, 44, 49, 54) sts.

Work in pattern until sleeve opening is 5.75 (6.25, 7.25, 7.75, 8.75, 9.25)", ending with a WS row. Body is approximately 23 (24, 25, 25.5, 26.5, 27)". BO 7 (9, 9, 11, 12, 13) sts at the beginning of the next 3 RS rows. BO all sts.

Back
Work same as Front through Sleeve Extension instructions. Work in pattern until sleeve opening is 4.75 (5.25, 5.75, 6, 7, 7.25)", ending with a WS row. Body is approximately 22 (23, 23.5, 23.75, 24.75, 25)".

Divide Neck
Next Row (RS): K39 (44, 48, 55, 60, 66), BO 17 (19, 21, 19, 19, 19) sts, K to end. 39 (44, 48, 55, 60, 66) sts for each front. Place right back sts onto holder.

Left Back
P 1 row. BO 3 (3, 3, 4, 4, 4) sts, then 3 sts, then 2 sts, at the beginning of the next RS rows. 31 (36, 40, 46, 51, 57) sts.

Sizes 43, 48, 53, 58 Only:
P 1 row.
Neck Dec Row (RS): K1, SSK, K to end. 1 st dec.
Rep Neck Dec Row every RS row - (-, 0, 1, 1, 2) more times. - (-, 39, 44, 49, 54) sts.

All Sizes: Work in pattern until sleeve opening is 5.75 (6.25, 7.25, 7.75, 8.75, 9.25)", ending with a RS row. Body is approximately 23 (24, 25, 25.5, 26.5, 27)". BO 7 (9, 9, 11, 12, 13) sts at the beginning of the next 3 WS rows. BO all sts.

Right Back
Place held right back sts onto needle with WS facing. BO 3 (3, 3, 4, 4, 4) sts, then 3 sts, then 2 sts, at the beginning of the next WS rows. 31 (36, 40, 46, 51, 57) sts.

Sizes 43, 48, 53, 58 Only:
Neck Dec Row (RS): K to last 3 sts, K2tog, K1. 1 st dec.
Rep Neck Dec Row every RS row - (-, 0, 1, 1, 2) more times. - (-, 39, 44, 49, 54) sts.

All Sizes: Work in pattern until sleeve opening is 5.75 (6.25, 7.25, 7.75, 8.75, 9.25)", ending with a WS row. Body is approximately 23 (24, 25, 25.5, 26.5, 27)". BO 7 (9, 9, 11, 12, 13) sts at the beginning of the next 3 RS rows. BO all sts.

Finishing
Weave in ends, wash and block to diagram. Sew shoulder and side seams.

Neckband:
With smaller needles, beginning at shoulder seam, PU & K 88 (92, 100, 104, 104, 108) sts around neck. PM and join for working in the rnd.

Rnd 1: P.
Rnd 1: K.
Rep Rnds 1-2 once more. BO all sts P-wise.

Sleeve Band (make 2):
With smaller needles, beginning at side seam, PU & K 48 (52, 61, 66, 75, 79) sts around sleeve opening. PM and join for working in the round.
Rnd 1: P.
Rnd 1: K.
Rep Rnds 1-2 once more. BO all sts P-wise.

Weave in remaining ends.

Chart A

	11	10	9	8	7	6	5	4	3	2	1	
20	●										●	
	●				O	Λ	O				●	19
18	●										●	
	●			O	/			\	O		●	17
16	●										●	
	●		O	/					\	O	●	15
14	●										●	
	●	O	/						\	O	●	13
12	●										●	
	●	/			O		O		\		●	11
10	●										●	
	●	/			O		O		\		●	9
8	●										●	
	●				O	Λ	O				●	7
6	●										●	
	●			O	/			\	O		●	5
4	●										●	
	●		O	/					\	O	●	3
2	●										●	
	●	O	/						\	O	●	1

Chart B

	13	12	11	10	9	8	7	6	5	4	3	2	1	
12	●	●										●	●	
	●	●				O	Λ	O				●	●	11
10	●	●										●	●	
	●	●			O	/			\	O		●	●	9
8	●	●										●	●	
	●	●		O	/				\	O		●	●	7
6	●	●										●	●	
	●	●	O	/					\	O		●	●	5
4	●	●										●	●	
	●	●	/			O		O		\		●	●	3
2	●	●										●	●	
	●	●	/			O		O		\		●	●	1

Legend

knit
RS: knit stitch
WS: purl stitch

● **purl**
RS: purl stitch
WS: knit stitch

O **yo**
Yarn Over

ssk
Slip one stitch as if to knit. Slip another stitch as if to knit. Insert left-hand needle into front of these two stitches and knit them together.

k2tog
Knit two stitches together as one stitch

Λ **sl1 k2tog psso**
slip 1, k2tog, pass slip stitch over, k2tog

Chart C

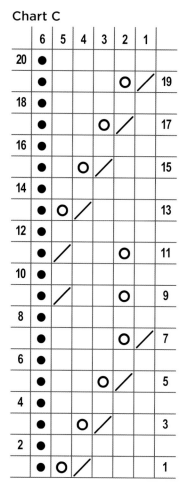

Row	6	5	4	3	2	1
20	●					
19	●				O	/
18	●					
17	●			O	/	
16	●					
15	●		O	/		
14	●					
13	●	O	/			
12	●					
11	●	/			O	
10	●					
9	●	/			O	
8	●					
7	●				O	/
6	●					
5	●			O	/	
4	●					
3	●		O	/		
2	●					
1	●	O	/			

Chart D

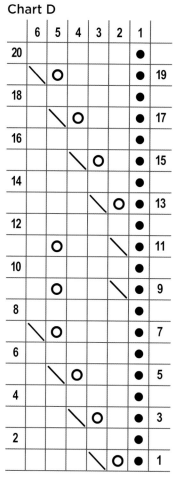

Row	6	5	4	3	2	1
20						●
19	\	O				●
18						●
17		\	O			●
16						●
15			\	O		●
14						●
13				\	O	●
12						●
11		O			\	●
10						●
9		O			\	●
8						●
7	\	O				●
6						●
5		\	O			●
4						●
3			\	O		●
2						●
1				\	O	●

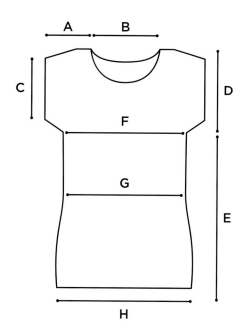

A 7.25 (8.25, 9, 10, 11.25, 12.25)"
B 7.25 (7.75, 8.75, 9, 9, 9.5)"
C 5.75 (6.25, 7.25, 7.75, 8.75, 9.25)"
D 6.75 (7.25, 8.25, 8.75, 9.75, 10.25)"
E 16.25 (16.75, 16.75, 16.75, 16.75, 16.75)"
F 17 (19.75, 22, 24.75, 27, 29.5)"
G 15.75 (18.5, 20.75, 23.25, 25.5, 28.25)"
H 18 (20.5, 23, 25.5, 28, 30.5)"

INVARIANCE

by M K Nance

FINISHED MEASUREMENTS
33 (37, 40.5, 44.5, 49, 52.5, 57, 59.75, 65)" finished bust measurements; meant to be worn with 1" of positive ease

YARN
Knit Picks Shine Sport Yarn
(60% Pima Cotton, 40% Modal® natural beech wood fiber; 110 yards/50g): Robot 25331, 10 (11, 12, 14, 15, 16, 17, 18, 19) balls.

NEEDLES
US 4 (3.5 mm) 32" or longer circular needles and DPNs or longer circular needle for Magic Loop technique, or size needed to obtain gauge

US 3 (3.25 mm) 32" or longer circular needles and DPNs or longer circular needle for Magic Loop technique, or one size smaller than size to obtain gauge

NOTIONS
4 locking stitch markers (or 2 locking stitch markers and 2 cable needles)
Waste yarn or stitch holder
Tapestry needle
6 (7, 7, 8, 8, 8, 9, 9, 9) buttons, .0.5" diameter

GAUGE
24 sts and 27 rows = 4" in St st worked flat on larger needles, blocked

For pattern support, contact
mknanceknit@gmail.com

Notes:

Invariance is the property of remaining unchanged regardless of situation. The cardigan features set in sleeves and is knit top down. There is no waist shaping. Starting at the nape of the neck there is one reverse Stockinette triangle which is almost the whole neckline. The sides of the triangle are outlined by decreases and yarn overs whose lines extend all the way to the sides for a little added interest. Under the crew neck line on the front of the cardigan there are the same triangles but shrunken and stacked with the lines extending only to the midline.

There is one cable in the whole sweater. It may be easier to use two locking stitch markers instead of two cable needles.

When working from the Back Chart, start on the row marked with the color for your size, working the sts outlined for your size.

Read the charts RS rows (odd numbers) from right to left, and WS rows (even numbers) from left to right.

Wrap and Turn (W&T)
Work until the stitch to be wrapped.
If knitting, bring the yarn to the front of the work, slip next stitch as if to purl, return the yarn to the back; turn work and slip wrapped st onto the RH needle. Continue across the row. If purling, bring yarn to the back of work, slip next stitch as if to purl, return the yarn to the front; turn work and slip wrapped st onto RH needle. Continue across the row.

Picking up Wraps
Work to the wrapped st.
If knitting, insert the RH needle under the wrap, then through the wrapped st K-wise. K the st and the wrap together.
If purling, slip the wrapped st P-wise onto the RH needle, and use the LH needle to lift the wrap and place it on the RH needle. Sl the wrap and the st back on the LH needle and P together.

1/1/1 LC: Sl1 to first CN and hold to front, Sl1 to second CN and hold to back, K1, K1 from second CN from back, K1 from first CN from front.

M1L (Make 1 Left Leaning Stitch): PU the bar between st just worked and the next st on needle as a regular st, inserting needle from front to back; K TBL.

M1R (Make 1 Right Leaning Stitch): PU the bar between st just worked and the next st on needle as an incorrectly mounted st, inserting needle from back to front; K through the front loop.

DIRECTIONS

Back
With larger needles CO 75 (81, 89, 101, 107, 113, 131, 139, 149).
Row 1 (WS): P.
Row 2 (RS): K21 (22, 24, 28, 29, 30, 38, 41, 46), PM, work 33 (37, 41, 45, 49, 53, 55, 57, 57) from the Back Chart using the first row marked for your size, PM, K4 (5, 6, 8, 8, 8, 11, 12, 14), W&T.
Row 3: P to M, SM, work next row of Back Chart, SM, K4 (5, 6, 8, 8, 8, 11, 12, 14), W&T.

Row 4: K to M, SM, work next row of Back Chart, SM, K to wrapped st, PU wrapped st, K4 (5, 6, 8, 8, 8, 11, 12, 14), W&T.
Row 5: P to M, SM, work next row of Back Chart, SM, P to wrapped st, PU wrapped st, P4 (5, 6, 8, 8, 8, 11, 12, 14), W&T.
Row 6: K to M, SM, work next row of Back Chart, SM, K to wrapped st, PU wrapped st, K to end.
Row 7: P to M, SM, work next row of Back Chart, SM, P to wrapped st, PU wrapped st, P to end.
Row 8: K to M, SM, work next row of Back Chart, SM, K to end.
Row 9: P to M, SM, work next row of Back Chart, SM, P to end.
Rep Rows 8-9 until back measures 6.75 (6, 6, 6.25, 6, 5.75, 7.75, 8, 8.25)" along armhole, ending with a WS row.

Shape Armholes
Row 1 (RS): K2, M1R, K to M, SM, work next row in Back Chart, SM, K to last 2 sts, M1L, K2.
Row 2 (WS): P to M, SM, work next row in Back Chart, SM, P to end.
Rep Rows 1-2 2 (4, 6, 6, 8, 11, 7, 9, 10) times total.
Next Row(RS): CO 4 sts, work as established to end.
Next Row(WS): CO 4 sts, work as established to end. 87 (97, 109, 121, 131, 143, 153, 165, 177) sts.
Place Back sts on waste yarn or stitch holder.

Right Front
With larger needles PU & K 21 (22, 24, 28, 29, 30, 38, 41, 46) sts from shoulder edge to edge of Back Chart.
Row 1 (WS): P4 (5, 6, 8, 8, 8, 11, 12, 14), W&T.
Row 2: K.
Row 3: P to wrapped st, PU wrapped st, P4 (5, 6, 8, 8, 8, 11, 12, 14), W&T.
Row 4: K.
Row 5: P to wrapped st, PU wrapped st, P4 (5, 6, 8, 8, 8, 11, 12, 14), W&T.
Row 6: K.
Row 7: P to wrapped st, PU wrapped st, P to end.
Work in St st for 2 (4, 2, 4, 6, 4, 6, 6, 6) rows ending with a WS row.

Shape Neck
Row 1 (RS): K to last 2 sts, M1R, K2.
Row 2 (WS): P.
Work Rows 1-2 1 (1, 1, 1, 2, 2, 3, 3, 3) times total. 22 (23, 25, 29, 31, 32, 41, 44, 49) sts.
Row 3: K to end, CO 2 sts at neck edge.
Row 4: P.
Work Rows 3-4 1 (2, 2, 2, 2, 2, 3, 2, 3) times total. 24 (27, 29, 33, 35, 36, 47, 48, 55) sts.
Row 5: K to end, CO 3 sts at neck edge.
Row 6: P.
Work Rows 5-6 1 (1, 1, 1, 2, 2, 2, 2, 3) times total. 27 (30, 32, 36, 41, 42, 53, 54, 64) sts.
Next Row: K to end, CO 10 (10, 10, 12, 12, 13, 12, 11, 10) sts. 37 (40, 42, 48, 53, 55, 65, 65, 74) sts.
Work 3 rows in St st.

Sizes 33, 37 and 40.5" use Front Small Right Chart while the remaining sizes use the Front Large Right Chart.

Next Row (RS): K21 (24, 26, 28, 33, 35, 45, 45, 54), PM, work 13 (13, 13, 17, 17, 17, 17, 17, 17) in Front Right Chart, PM, K3.

Next Row (WS): P3, SM, work next row in Front Right Chart, SM, P to end.

Work as est until Right Front measures 6.75 (6, 6, 6.25, 6, 5.75, 7.75, 8, 8.25)" along armhole, ending with a WS row.

Shape Armhole

Row 1 (RS): K2, M1R, K to M, SM, work next row in Front Right Chart, SM, K3.

Row 2 (WS): P to M, SM, work next row in Front Right Chart, SM, P to end.

Rep Rows 1-2 2 (4, 6, 6, 8, 11, 7, 9, 10) times total. 39 (44, 48, 54, 61, 66, 72, 74, 84) sts.

Next Row(RS): CO 4 sts, work as established to end. 43 (48, 52, 58, 65, 70, 76, 78, 88) sts.

Next Row(WS): Work as established to end.

Place Right Front sts on waste yarn or stitch holder.

Left Front

With larger needles PU & K from edge of Back Chart to shoulder edge 21 (22, 24, 28, 29, 30, 38, 41, 46) sts.

Row 1: P.

Row 2: K4 (5, 6, 8, 8, 8, 11, 12, 14), W&T.

Row 3: P.

Row 4: K to wrapped st, PU wrapped st, K4 (5, 6, 8, 8, 8, 11, 12, 14), W&T.

Row 5: P.

Row 6: K to wrapped st, PU wrapped st, K4 (5, 6, 8, 8, 8, 11, 12, 14), W&T.

Row 8: P.

Row 9: K to wrapped st, PU wrapped st, K to end.

Work in St st for 1 (3, 1, 3, 5, 3, 5, 5, 5) rows ending with a WS row.

Shape Neck

Row 1 (RS): K2, M1L, K to end.

Row 2 (WS): P.

Work Rows 1-2 1(1, 1, 1, 2, 2, 3, 3, 3) times total. 22 (23, 25, 29, 31, 32, 41, 44, 49) sts.

Row 3 (RS): CO 2 sts at neck edge, K to end.

Row 4 (WS): P.

Work Rows 3-4 1 (2, 2, 2, 2, 2, 3, 2, 3) times total. 24 (27, 29, 33, 35, 36, 47, 48, 55) sts.

Row 5 (RS): CO 3 sts at neck edge, K to end.

Row 6 (WS): P.

Work Rows 5-6 1(1, 1, 1, 2, 2, 2, 2, 3) times total. 27 (30, 32, 36, 41, 42, 53, 54, 64) sts.

Next Row (RS): CO 10 (10, 10, 12, 12, 13, 12, 11, 10) sts, K to end. 37 (40, 42, 48, 53, 55, 65, 65, 74) sts.

Work 3 rows in St st.Sizes 33, 37 and 40.5" use Front Small Left Chart while the remaining sizes use the Front Large Left Chart.

Next Row (RS): K3, PM, work 13 (13, 13, 17, 17, 17, 17, 17, 17) in Front Left Chart, PM, K to end.

Next Row (WS): P to M, SM, work next row in Front Left Chart, SM, P3.

Work as est until front measures 6.75 (6, 6, 6.25, 6, 5.75, 7.75, 8, 8.25)" along armhole, ending with a WS row.

Shape Armhole

Row 1 (RS): K to M, SM, work next row in Front Left Chart, SM, K to last 2 sts, M1L, K2.

Row 2 (WS): P to M, SM, work next row in Front Left Chart, SM, P to end.

Repeat Rows 1-2 2 (4, 6, 6, 8, 11, 7, 9, 10) times total. 39 (44, 48, 54, 61, 66, 72, 74, 84) sts.

Next Row(RS): Work as established to end, CO4 sts. 43 (48, 52, 58, 65, 70, 76, 78, 88) sts.

Next Row(WS): Work as established to end.

Lower Body

Starting with Left Front work across in pattern as established, using a knitted CO, CO 5 (6, 6, 6, 7, 6, 8, 8, 8), PM to mark underarm, using a knitted CO, CO 5 (6, 6, 6, 7, 7, 8, 8, 8), join Back and work in pattern, using a knitted CO, CO 5 (6, 6, 6, 7, 7, 8, 8, 8), PM to mark underarm, using a knitted CO, CO 5 (6, 6, 6, 7, 6, 8, 8, 8), join Right Front, and work across in pattern to end. 193 (217, 237, 261, 289, 309, 337, 353, 385) sts

Work in pattern until piece measures 12 (12.5, 12.5, 13.5, 13.75, 14.25, 14, 14.25, 14.5)" from armhole or 1.5 (2, 2, 2, 2, 2.5, 2.5, 2.5, 2.5)" less than desired length ending with Row 12 (12, 12, 16, 16, 16, 16, 16, 16) or Row 24 (24, 24, 32, 32, 32, 32, 32, 32) of Front Charts.

Note:

For the Back pattern, after working Back Chart Row 92 (96, 100, 104, 106, 106, 106, 106, 106) remove markers and continue in pattern as follows:

RS Rows: K to 1 st before last RS K2tog, YO, K to last RS YO, K1, YO, SSK, K to end.

WS Rows: P.

Switch to smaller needles

Next Row (RS): K1, KFB, (P2, K2) rep to end. 194 (218, 238, 262, 290, 310, 338, 354, 386) sts

Work in rib pattern at established for 1.5 (2, 2, 2, 2.5, 2.5, 2.5, 2.5)". BO all sts.

Sleeves (work two)

With RS facing, starting at center of underarm, PU & K80 (80, 84, 86, 90, 92, 98, 104, 112) sts. PM and join in the rnd.

Short Row Shaping

Row 1(RS): K49 (49, 52, 53, 56, 57, 61, 64, 70), W&T.

Row 2(WS): P18 (18, 20, 20, 22, 22, 24, 24, 28), W&T.

Row 3 : K to wrapped st, PU wrap, K1, W&T.

Row 4: P to wrapped st, PU wrap, P1, W&T.

Repeat Rows 3-4 7 (4, 4, 4, 3, 3, 2, 2, 2) more times.

Next Row: K to wrapped st, PU wrap, W&T.

Next Row: P to wrapped st, PU wrap, W&T.

Repeat these last two rows 5 (6, 7, 8, 10, 11, 15, 17, 19) more times.

Next Row: K to wrapped st, PU wrap, K3, W&T.

Next Row: P to wrapped st, PU wrap, P3, W&T.

Next Row: K to wrapped st, PU wrap, K4 (5, 5, 5, 6, 6, 6, 7, 7), W&T.

Next Row: P to wrapped st, PU wrap, P4(5, 5, 5, 6, 6, 6, 7, 7), W&T.

Join in the rnd and work in St st until the sleeve measures 1.5" from the underarm.

Taper Sleeves

Dec Rnd: K1, K2tog, K to last 3 sts, SSK, K1.
Work Dec rnd every 8th round 0 (0, 0, 0, 2, 5, 6, 6, 7) times,
Work Dec rnd every 6th round 8 (8, 8, 9, 9, 5, 3, 4, 1) times.
64 (64, 68, 68, 68, 72, 80, 84, 96) sts

Work in St st in the rnd until sleeve reaches 9 (9.5, 9.5, 10, 10.5, 10.5, 10.5, 11, 11)" or 2.5" less than desired length.
Work in 2x2 Rib for 2.5". BO all sts loosely in pattern.

Right Buttonhole Band

PU & K 102 (102, 110, 114, 114, 126, 122, 130, 134) sts along neck line.
Row 1 (RS): (K2, P2) repeat to last two sts, K2.
Row 2 (WS): (P2, K2) repeat to the last two sts, P2.
Rep Rows 1-2 until band measures 0.25" ending with WS row.
Mark placement for buttonholes, placing one buttonhole 0.25" from top and another 0.5" from bottom, evenly pace the remaining buttonholes.
Next Row (RS): Cont in established pattern, BO 2 sts for buttonholes at each marker.
Next Row (WS): Cont in established pattern, CO 2 sts at each buttonhole over BO sts.
Work in pattern until measures 1" ending with RS row.
BO all in pattern.

Left Button Band

PU & K 102 (102, 110, 114, 114, 126, 122, 130, 134) sts along neck line.
Row 1 (RS): (K2, P2) repeat to last two sts, K2.
Row 2 (WS): (P2, K2) repeat to the last two sts, P2.
Work in pattern until measures 1" ending with RS row.
BO all in pattern.

Collar

With smaller needles PU & K 102 (102, 114, 122, 134, 138, 146, 154, 154) sts along neck line.
Row 1 (RS): (K2, P2) repeat to last two sts, K2.
Row 2 (WS): (P2, K2) repeat to the last two sts, P2.
Work in pattern until measures 1" ending with RS row.
BO all in pattern.

Finishing

Weave in ends. Block to measurement. Sew on buttons.

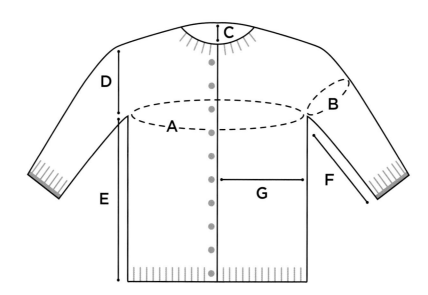

A 33 (37, 40.5, 44.5, 49, 52.5, 57, 59.75, 65)"
B 13.25 (13.25, 14, 14.25, 15, 15.25, 16.25, 17.25, 18.75)"
C 1.75 (2.5, 2.5, 2.5, 3, 3, 3.25, 3.25, 3.25)"
D 7.5 (7.5, 8, 8.25, 8.75, 9.25, 10.25, 11, 11.5)"
E 13.5 (14.5, 14.5, 15.5, 15.75, 16.25, 16.5, 16.75, 17)"
F 11.5 (12, 12, 12.5, 12.5, 13, 13, 13.5 13.5)"
G 9 (10, 11, 12, 13, 14, 15, 16, 17)"

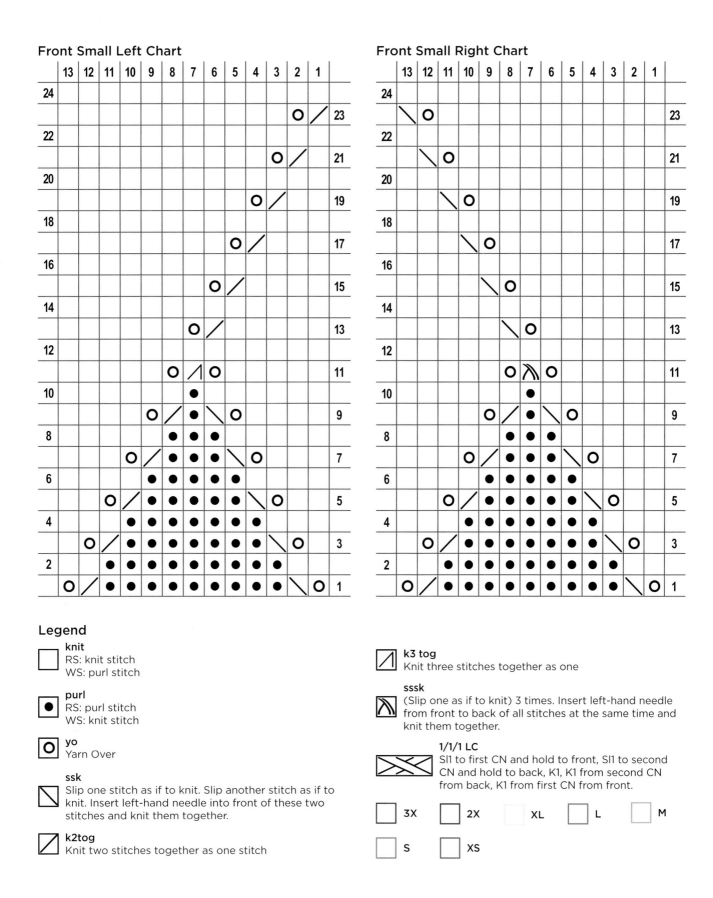

Front Small Left Chart

Front Small Right Chart

Legend

knit
RS: knit stitch
WS: purl stitch

purl
RS: purl stitch
WS: knit stitch

yo
Yarn Over

ssk
Slip one stitch as if to knit. Slip another stitch as if to knit. Insert left-hand needle into front of these two stitches and knit them together.

k2tog
Knit two stitches together as one stitch

k3 tog
Knit three stitches together as one

sssk
(Slip one as if to knit) 3 times. Insert left-hand needle from front to back of all stitches at the same time and knit them together.

1/1/1 LC
Sl1 to first CN and hold to front, Sl1 to second CN and hold to back, K1, K1 from second CN from back, K1 from first CN from front.

| 3X | 2X | XL | L | M |
| S | XS |

Front Large Left Chart

Row	17	16	15	14	13	12	11	10	9	8	7	6	5	4	3	2	1	Row
32																		
															O	/		31
30																		
														O	/			29
28																		
													O	/				27
26																		
												O	/					25
24																		
											O	/						23
22																		
										O	/							21
20																		
									O	/								19
18																		
								O	/									17
16																		
								O	⋏	O								15
14									•									
							O	/	•	\	O							13
12								•	•	•								
						O	/	•	•	•	\	O						11
10							•	•	•	•	•							
					O	/	•	•	•	•	•	\	O					9
8						•	•	•	•	•	•							
				O	/	•	•	•	•	•	•	•	\	O				7
6					•	•	•	•	•	•	•	•	•					
			O	/	•	•	•	•	•	•	•	•	•	\	O			5
4				•	•	•	•	•	•	•	•	•	•	•				
		O	/	•	•	•	•	•	•	•	•	•	•	•	\	O		3
2			•	•	•	•	•	•	•	•	•	•	•	•	•			
	O	/	•	•	•	•	•	•	•	•	•	•	•	•	•	\	O	1

Front Large Right Chart

17	16	15	14	13	12	11	10	9	8	7	6	5	4	3	2	1	Row
																	32
\	O																31
																	30
	\	O															29
																	28
		\	O														27
																	26
			\	O													25
																	24
				\	O												23
																	22
					\	O											21
																	20
						\	O										19
																	18
							\	O									17
																	16
						O	⋀	O									15
								●									14
						O	/	●	\	O							13
								●	●	●							12
					O	/	●	●	●	\	O						11
							●	●	●	●							10
				O	/	●	●	●	●	●	\	O					9
					●	●	●	●	●	●							8
			O	/	●	●	●	●	●	●	●	\	O				7
				●	●	●	●	●	●	●	●						6
		O	/	●	●	●	●	●	●	●	●	●	\	O			5
			●	●	●	●	●	●	●	●	●	●					4
	O	/	●	●	●	●	●	●	●	●	●	●	●	\	O		3
		●	●	●	●	●	●	●	●	●	●	●	●				2
O	/	●	●	●	●	●	●	●	●	●	●	●	●	●	\	O	1

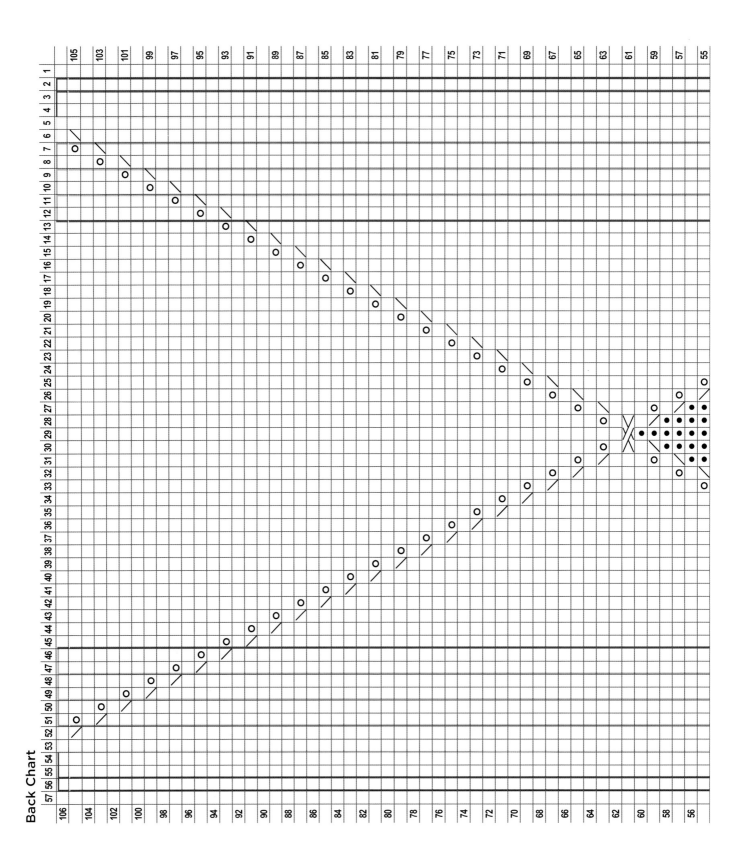

Back Chart

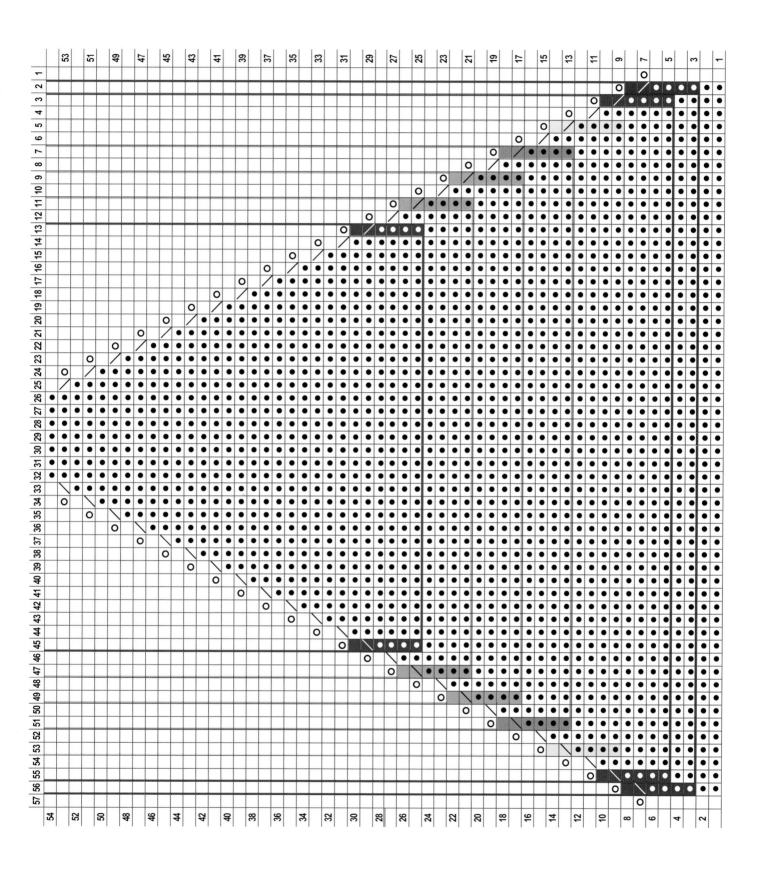

JUNE TANK

by Ann L. Albe

FINISHED MEASUREMENTS

35.75 (37.75, 39.5, 42.25, 44.25)" finished bust measurement; garment is meant to be worn with 4" of positive ease

YARN

Knit Picks CotLin DK
(70% Tanguis Cotton, 30% Linen; 123 yards/50g): Hydrangea 25772, 4 (5, 5, 5, 6) balls

NEEDLES

US 5 (3.75mm) 24" circular needles, or one size smaller than size to obtain gauge
US 6 (4mm) 24" circular needles, or size to obtain gauge

NOTIONS

Yarn Needle
Stitch Markers
Scrap yarn or stitch holder

GAUGE

17 sts and 24 rows = 4" in St st on larger needles, blocked

For pattern support, contact theknottingway@gmail.com

Notes:

June is a loose, sleeveless boat neck top, knit in the round from the bottom up with subtle waist shaping. It features Cat's Eye Lace stitch details at the hem and at the front neckline. The Cat's Eye Lace stitch is found in historic shawls from Ireland, Scotland, and Wales and adds a vintage twist to this contemporary design. Lightweight and comfortable, June is a versatile garment.

Alternating Cable Cast On

Step 1: Make a slip knot and place on LH needle.

Step 2: Insert RH needle into st K-wise and pull new st through and place on the LH needle.

Step 3: Insert RH needle between the last 2 sts on the LH needle from front to back, pull new st through and place on LH needle.

Step 4: Insert RH needle between the last 2 sts on the LH needle from back to front and pull new st through and place on LH needle.

Rep Steps 3-4 until desired number of sts are cast on.

DIRECTIONS

Body

With larger circular needles CO 152 (160, 168, 180, 188) sts using the Alternating Cable Cast On. PM and join for working in the rnd, being careful not to twist sts.

Rnd 1: K.

Rnd 2: P.

Rep Rnds 1-2 once more.

Knit 2 rnds.

Bottom Cat's Eye Lace Detail

Rnd 1: K2, *YO twice, K4; rep from * to last 2 sts, YO twice, K2.

Rnd 2: *K2tog, (K1, P1) into double YO of previous rnd, K2tog; rep from* to end.

Rnd 3: *K4, YO twice; rep from* to end.

Rnd 4: *K2tog twice, (K1, P1) into double YO of previous rnd, rep from * to end.

Move BOR M 1 st to the right.

Work Rnds 1-4 of Bottom Cat's Eye Lace Detail two times total.

Continue in St st until piece measures 4.5 (4.75, 4.75, 4.75, 4.75)" from CO edge.

Waist shaping

Switch to smaller needle and continue to work in pattern until piece measures 9.5 (9.75, 10.75, 10.75, 10.75)" from CO edge.

Switch to larger needle size and continue to work in pattern until piece measures 16 (16.25, 16.75, 16.75, 16.75)" from CO edge.

Divide for Front and Back

Set Up Row: K76 (80, 84, 90, 94) sts, place remaining 76 (80, 84, 90, 94) sts on a holder, turn.

Next Row (WS): K4 (4, 4, 3, 3), P to last 4 (4, 4, 3, 3) sts, K4 (4, 4, 3, 3).

Front Armhole Shaping

Size 35.75" Only

Row 1 (RS): K4, K3tog, K2tog, K to last 9 sts, SSK, SSSK, K4. 6 sts dec.

Row 2 (WS): K4, P to last 4 sts, K4.

Rep Rows 1-2 once more.

Row 5: K4, K3tog, K to last 7 sts, SSSK, K4. 4 sts dec.

Row 6: K4, P to last 4 sts, K4. 60 sts.

Sizes 37.75 & 39.5" Only

Row 1 (RS): K4, K3tog, K3tog, K to last 10 sts, SSSK, SSSK, K4. 8 sts dec.

Rows 2, 4, 6, & 8 (WS): K4, P to last 4 sts, K4.

Row 3: K4, K3tog, K2tog, K to last 9 sts, SSK, SSSK, K4. 6 sts dec.

Row 5: K4, K3tog, K to last 7 sts, SSSK, K4. 4 sts dec.

Row 7: K4, K2tog, K to last 6 sts, SSK, K4. 2 sts dec. 60 (64) sts.

Sizes 42.25 & 44.25" Only

Row 1 (RS): K3, K3tog, K3tog, K2tog, K to last 11 sts, SSK, SSSK, SSSK, K3. 10 sts dec.

Rows 2, 4, & 6 (WS): K3, P to last 3 sts, K3.

Row 3: K3, K3tog, K2tog, K to last 8 sts, SSK, SSSK, K3. 6 sts dec.

Row 5: K3, K3tog, K to last 6 sts, SSSK, K3. 4 sts dec.

Rep Rows 5-6 one more time. 66 (70) sts.

Front

Next Row (RS): K.

Next Row (WS): K4 (4, 4, 3, 3), P to last 4 (4, 4, 3, 3) sts, K4 (4, 4, 3, 3).

Rep last two rows until armhole measures 4 (4.5, 4.75, 5, 5.25)" ending with a WS row.

Front Cat's Eye Lace Panel

Row 1: K8 (8, 8, 7, 7), * YO twice, K4; rep from * to last 4 (4, 4, 3, 3) sts, K4 (4, 4, 3, 3).

Row 2: K4 (4, 4, 3, 3), P2, * P2tog, (P1, K1) into double YO of previous row, P2tog; rep from * until last 6 (6, 6, 5, 5) sts, P2, K4 (4, 4, 3, 3).

Row 3: K6 (6, 6, 5, 5), YO, * K4, YO twice; rep from * to last 10 (10, 10, 9, 9) sts, K4, YO, K6 (6, 6, 5, 5).

Row 4: K4 (4, 4, 3, 3), P3, * P2tog twice, (P1, K1) into double YO of previous row, rep from * until last 11 (11, 11, 10, 10) sts, P2tog twice, P3, K4 (4, 4, 3, 3).

Rep Front Cat's Eye Lace Panel Rows 1-4 two times total.

Next Row (RS): K.

Next Row (WS): K4 (4, 4, 3, 3), P to last 4 (4, 4, 3, 3) sts, K4 (4, 4, 3, 3).

Rep last two rows until armhole measures 6.5 (7, 7.25, 7.5, 7.75)" ending with a WS row.

Neck Edging Front

Knit 6 rows. BO all sts.

Back

Place held sts back on larger needle. Join yarn with RS facing and work Armhole Shaping as for Front.

Next Row (RS): K.

Next Row: K4 (4, 4, 3, 3), P to last 4 (4, 4, 3, 3) sts, K4 (4, 4, 3, 3). Work in established pattern until armhole measures 6.5 (7, 7.25, 7.5, 7.75)" ending with a WS row.

Neck Edging Back
Knit 6 rows. BO all sts.

Finishing
With RS facing, seam 9 (10, 10, 10, 10) shoulder sts together on each shoulder. Weave in ends, block to measurements.

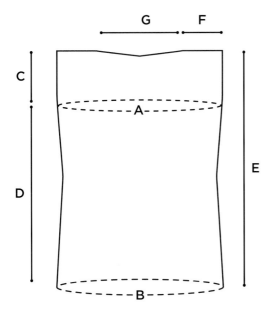

A 35.75 (37.75, 39.5, 42.25, 42.26)"
B 35.75 (37.75, 39.5, 42.25, 44.26)"
C 7 (7.5, 7.75, 8, 8.25)"
D 16 (16.25, 16.75, 16.75, 16.75)"
E 23 (23.75, 24.5, 24.75, 25)"
F 2 (2.25, 2.25, 2.25, 2.25)"
G 10 (9.5, 10.25, 10.75, 11.75)"

VINTAGE VEE TEE

by Cassie Castillo

FINISHED MEASUREMENTS

34.25 (37.25, 40.5, 43.5, 46.5, 49.5, 52.5, 55.75, 58.75)" finished bust measurement; garment is meant to be worn with 0-1" ease.

YARN

Knit Picks Comfy Sport
(75% Pima Cotton, 25% Acrylic; 136 yards/50g) Ivory 24429, 5 (6, 6, 7, 8, 8, 9, 9, 10) balls

NEEDLES

US 4 (3.5 mm) straight or circular needles, or size to obtain gauge
US 3 (3.25 mm) DPNs and/or 16" circular needles or two 24" circular needles for two circulars technique, or one 32" or longer circular needle for Magic Loop technique, for ribbing at hem, armband, and neckband, or one size smaller than size to obtain gauge

NOTIONS

Yarn Needle
Stitch Markers
Locking stitch markers
Scrap yarn or stitch holders

GAUGE

21 sts and 28 rows= 4" in St st on larger needles, blocked
8 sts and 12 rows= 1.5" over one repeats of Cat's Paw chart on larger needles, blocked

Notes:

The Vintage Vee Tee is worked flat in pieces from the bottom up. The length measurements in the pattern reflect the blocked length; adjust the length if your blocked and unblocked gauges are different.

Left Lifted Increase (LLI):

K 1 into the st below the previously worked st on the right needle.

Right Lifted Increase (RLI):

K 1 into the st below the next st on the left needle.

DIRECTIONS

Front

With smaller needles, CO 98 (106, 114, 122, 130, 138, 146, 154, 162) sts.

Row 1 (RS): *K2, P2; rep from * to last 2 sts, K2.

Row 2 (WS): *P2, K2; rep from * to last 2 sts, P2.

Rep Row 1-2 until Ribbing is 1.5", ending with a WS row. Change to larger needles.

Next Row (RS): K.

Next Row (WS): P.

Dec Row (RS): K1, SSK, K to last 3 sts, K2tog, K1. 2 sts dec. Cont in St st as established, repeating Dec Row every 6th row 4 more times, then every 4th row 3 times. 82 (90, 98, 106, 114, 122, 130, 138, 146) sts.

Work in St st until piece measures 7.25 (7.5, 7.25, 7.5, 7.5, 7.75, 7.5, 7.75, 7.5)" from CO edge, ending with a WS row.

Cat's Paw

Row 1 (RS): K1, work Cat's Paw Chart to last st, K1.

Row 2 (WS): P1, work Cat's Paw Chart to last st, P1.

Rep Rows 1-2 until Rows 1-12 of Cat's Paw Chart are complete.

Inc Row (RS): K1, RLI, K to last st, LLI, K1. 2 sts inc. Work in St st and rep Inc Row every 6th row 4 more times. 92 (100, 108, 116, 124, 132, 140, 148, 156) sts.

Armhole shaping begins with or before the Neckline Motif Chart for largest sizes. Read through the following section before beginning.

Neckline Motif

When piece measures 13.25 (13.75, 13.75, 14.25, 14.25, 14.75, 14.75, 15.25, 15.25)" from CO edge, on a RS row work Neckline Motif Chart over center 40 sts, placing M on both sides of center sts. After Row 1, Neckline Motif decreases to 39 sts, and total st count loses one st.

Cont in pattern until Rows 1-36 of Neckline Motif Chart are complete. Piece is approximately 17.75 (18.25, 18.25, 18.75, 18.75, 19.25, 19.25, 19.75, 19.75)".

Armhole Shaping

At the same time, when piece measures 14.5 (14.5, 14.5, 14.5, 14.5, 14.5, 14.5, 14.5, 14.25)" from CO edge, ending with a WS row, BO 4 (4, 5, 5, 6, 6, 7, 7, 8) sts at the beginning of the next 2 rows.

Armhole Dec Row (RS): K1, SSK, work in pattern to last 3 sts, K2tog, K1. 2 sts dec.

Armhole Dec Row (WS): P1, P2tog, work in pattern to last 3 sts, SSP, P1. 2 sts dec.

Work a Dec Row every row 6 (6, 8, 8, 8, 10, 10, 12, 12) times total, then RS Dec Row every other row 4 (6, 5, 7, 8, 8, 9, 9, 10) times. 63 (67, 71, 75, 79, 83, 87, 91, 95) sts.

Divide Neck:

Next Row (RS): K12 (12, 16, 16, 16, 20, 20, 24, 24) and place on holder for Left Front, K39 (43, 39, 43, 47, 43, 47, 43, 47) and place on holder for neckband, K to end. 12 (12, 16, 16, 16, 20, 20, 24, 24) sts rem for Right Front.

Right Front

P 1 row.

Sizes 34.25, 37.25, 49.5, 52.5" only:

Next Row (RS): K2, work Cat's Paw Chart to last 2 sts, K2.

Next Row (WS): P2, work Cat's Paw Chart to last 2 sts, P2.

Sizes 40.5, 43.5, 46.5, 55.75, 58.75" only:

Next Row (RS): K2, work Cat's Paw Right Chart, work Cat's Paw Chart to last 2 sts, K2.

Next Row (WS): P2, work Cat's Paw Chart, work Cat's Paw Right Chart to last 2 sts, P2.

All Sizes:

Cont in established pattern until armhole is 7.75 (8.25, 8.5, 9, 9.25, 9.75, 10, 10.5, 10.75)", ending with a WS row. BO all sts.

Left Front

Place 12 (12, 16, 16, 16, 20, 20, 24, 24) held sts onto needle with WS facing. P 1 row.

Sizes 34.25, 37.25, 49.5, 52.5" only:

Next Row (RS): K2, work Cat's Paw Chart to last 2 sts, K2.

Next Row (WS): P2, work Cat's Paw Chart to last 2 sts, P2.

Sizes 40.5, 43.5, 46.5, 55.75, 58.75" only:

Next Row (RS): K2, work Cat's Paw Chart, work Cat's Paw Left Chart to last 6 sts, K2.

Next Row (WS): P2, work Cat's Paw Left Chart, work Cat's Paw Chart to last 2 sts, P2.

All Sizes:

Cont in established pattern until armhole is 7.75 (8.25, 8.5, 9, 9.25, 9.75, 10, 10.5, 10.75)", ending with a WS row. BO all sts.

Back

Work same as Front, omitting Neckline Motif Chart, until piece measures 17.75 (18.25, 18.25, 18.75, 18.75, 19.25, 19.25, 19.75, 19.75)" from CO edge. 64 (68, 72, 76, 80, 84, 88, 92, 96) sts.

Cont in pattern until piece measures 19.75 (20.25, 20.25, 20.75, 20.75, 21.25, 21.25, 21.75, 21.75)" from CO edge, ending with a WS row.

Divide Neck:

Next Row (RS): K12 (12, 16, 16, 16, 20, 20, 24, 24) and place on holder for Right Back, K40 (44, 40, 44, 48, 44, 48, 44, 48) and place on holder for Neckline, K to end. 12 (12, 16, 16, 16, 20, 20, 24, 24) sts rem for Left Back.

Left Back
Work same as Right Front.

Right Back
Work same as Left Front.

Finishing
Weave in ends, wash and block to diagram. Sew shoulder and side seams.

Arm band:
With smaller circular needles, beginning at side seam, pick up and knit 80 (88, 92, 96, 100, 108, 112, 116, 120) sts. PM and join for working in the round.

Next Rnd: *K2, P2; rep from * to end.
Cont in pat until rib is .75". BO all sts in pat.

Neckband:
With smaller circular needles, beginning at left shoulder seam, PU & K 22 (22, 24, 24, 24, 24, 26, 26, 26) sts along strap to neckline, place locking M on last st, K across held 39 (43, 39, 43, 47, 43, 47, 43, 47) sts for front neck, place locking M on last st, PU & K 33 (33, 37, 37, 39, 39, 41, 41, 41) sts along right strap to back neck, place locking M on last st, K across held 40 (44, 40, 44, 48, 44, 48, 44, 48) sts for back neck, place locking M on last st, PU & K 10 (10, 12, 12, 14, 14, 14, 14, 14) sts along back strap to shoulder seam. 144 (152, 152, 160, 172, 164, 176, 168, 176) sts. PM and join for working in the rnd.

Rnd 1: *K2, P2; rep from * to end. Move locking markers up one rnd.

Rnd 2: *Work in pattern to 1 st before M, Sk2p; rep from * 3 more times, work in pattern to end. 4 sts dec. Move locking markers up one rnd.

Rep Rnds 1-2 until Ribbing is .75". BO all sts in pattern.

Weave in remaining ends.

Cat's Paw Chart

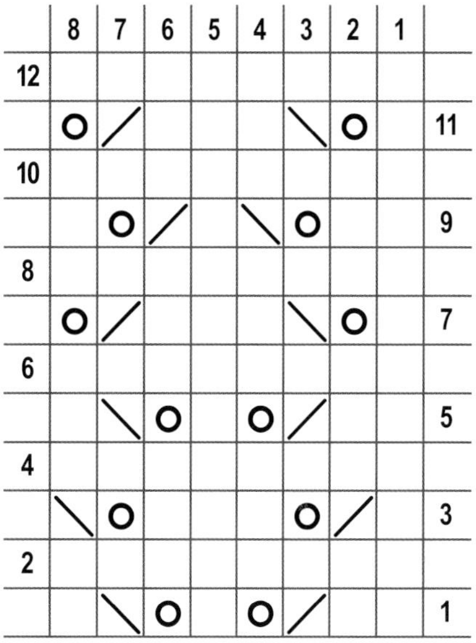

	8	7	6	5	4	3	2	1	
12									
	O	/				\	O		11
10									
		O	/		\	O			9
8									
	O	/				\	O		7
6									
			\	O		O	/		5
4									
		\	O			O	/		3
2									
			\	O		O	/		1

Legend

☐ **knit**
RS: knit stitch
WS: purl stitch

⊙ **yo**
Yarn Over

⧄ **k2tog**
Knit two stitches together as one stitch

⧅ **ssk**
Slip one stitch as if to knit. Slip another stitch as if to knit. Insert left-hand needle into front of these two stitches and knit them together.

Neckline Motif Chart

Column numbers (left to right): 39 38 37 36 35 34 33 32 31 30 29 28 27 26 25 24 23 22 21 20 19 18 17 16 15 14 13 12 11 10 9 8 7 6 5 4 3 2 1

Row numbers (left, even): 36 34 32 30 28 26 24 22 20 18 16 14 12 10 8 6 4 2

Row numbers (right, odd): 35 33 31 29 27 25 23 21 19 17 15 13 11 9 7 5 3 1

Cat's Paw Left Chart

	4	3	2	1	
12					
		\	O		11
10					
		\	O		9
8					
		\	O		7
6					
	O	/			5
4					
		O	/		3
2					
	O	/			1

Cat's Paw Right Chart

	4	3	2	1	
12					
	O	/			11
10					
		O	/		9
8					
	O	/			7
6					
		\	O		5
4					
	\	O			3
2					
		\	O		1

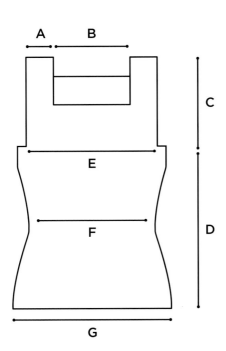

A 2.25 (2.25, 3, 3, 3, 3.75, 3.75, 4.5, 4.5)"

B 7.5 (8.5, 7.5, 8.5, 9.25, 8.5, 9.25, 8.5, 9.25)"

C 7.75 (8.25, 8.5, 9, 9.25, 9.75, 10, 10.5, 10.75)"

D 14.5 (14.5, 14.5, 14.5, 14.5, 14.5, 14.5, 14.5, 14.25)"

E 17.5 (19, 20.5, 22, 23.5, 25.25, 26.75, 28.25, 29.75)"

F 15.5 (17.25, 18.75, 20.25, 21.75, 23.25, 24.75, 26.25, 27.75)"

G 18.75 (20.25, 21.75, 23.25, 24.75, 26.25, 27.75, 29.25, 30.75)"

LACY SHOULDERS TEE

by Heather Storta

FINISHED MEASUREMENTS

31 (35, 39.5, 43.5, 47, 51, 55.5, 59.5, 63)"
finished bust measurement; garment is
meant to be worn with 1-2" of ease

YARN

Knit Picks Lindy Chain
(70% Linen, 30% Pima Cotton; 180
yards/50g): Plum 26462, 6 (7, 7, 8, 9, 10,
11, 12, 13) balls

NEEDLES

US 3 (3.25mm) straight or circular
needles, or size to obtain gauge
US 2 (2.75mm) straight or circular
needles, or size to obtain gauge

NOTIONS

Yarn Needle
Stitch Markers (removeable)
Scrap yarn or stitch holder

GAUGE

29 sts and 41 rows = 4" in St st, on larger
needles, blocked
29 sts and 60 rows = 4" in Seed st on
smaller needles, blocked
25 sts and 38 rows = 4" in German
Honeycomb Lace on larger needles, blocked

Notes:

This A-line and airy tee is knit in one piece from the bottom front hem to the back hem. The sides are then seamed and the neckline is picked up and worked in Seed stitch. The lace at the shoulders is patterned every row, but easily memorized and not difficult. This breezy top is sure to be a spring and summer favorite!

Seed Stitch (worked flat over odd number of sts)

Row 1: (K1, P1) across to last st, K1.
Rep Row 1 for pattern.

Seed Stitch (worked in the rnd over even number of sts)

Rnd 1: (K1, P1) to end.
Rnd 2: (P1, K1) to end.
Rep Rnds 1-2 for pattern.

German Honeycomb Lace (worked flat over multiple of 4 plus 4 sts)

Row 1 (RS): *K2tog, YO, SSK; rep from * to end.
Row 2 (WS): P1, *(K1, P1) into the YO of previous row, P2; rep from * to last 2 sts, (K1, P1) in the YO of previous row, P1.
Row 3: K.
Row 4: P2, *P2togTBL, YO, P2tog; rep from * to last 2 sts, P2.
Row 5: K3, *(K1, P1) into the YO of previous row, K2; rep from * to last st, K1.
Row 6: P.
Rep Rows 1-6 for pattern.

Purl 2 Together, Slip, Pass (P2SP)

P2tog, slip next st K-wise to right needle. Using left needle, slip first st over the second. 2 sts dec.

DIRECTIONS

Front

The sweater is worked in one piece from the front hem to the back hem.

Hem

Using smaller needles, CO 123 (137, 151, 165, 179, 193, 207, 221, 237) sts. Work in Seed st until piece measures 1" from CO edge, ending with a WS row.
Switch to larger needles.
Setup Row (RS): Work 5 sts in Seed st, K56 (63, 70, 77, 84, 91, 98, 105, 113), P1, K to last 5 sts, work 5 sts in Seed st.
Next Row (WS): Work 5 sts in Seed st, P56 (63, 70, 77, 84, 91, 98, 105, 113), K1, P to last 5 sts, work 5 sts in Seed st.
Work in established pattern with 5 Seed sts at beg and end of row and center st in rev St st for 1", ending with a WS row.
Selvedge Inc Row (RS): KFB, K to center st, P1, K to last st, KFB. 2 sts inc. 125 (139, 153, 167, 181, 195, 209, 223, 239) sts total.

Body Decreases

Using row markers will help while working this section.
*Work in St st, maintaining center rev St st, for 2 (2, 3, 3, 3, 3, 4, 4, 3)", ending with a WS row.
Dec Row (RS): K1, SSK, K to center st, P1, K to last 3 sts, K2tog, K1. 2 sts dec.
Rep from * 4 (4, 2, 2, 2, 2, 2, 2, 3) more times. 10 (10, 6, 6, 6, 6, 6, 6, 8) sts dec.

Sizes 39.5, 43.5, 47, and 51" only:

Work in St st, maintaining center rev St st, for 2", ending with a WS row. Then work Dec Row once more. 2 sts dec. 115 (129, 145, 159, 173, 187, 203, 217, 231) sts rem after all dec have been made.
Work in established pattern until piece measures 12 (13, 13, 13, 13, 13.5, 14, 14, 14)" from CO edge, ending with a WS row.

Sleeves and Neckline

Sleeve and Neckline shaping are worked at the same time. Read ahead to start the Neckline at the correct point.

Sleeve Increases

Inc Row (RS): K1, M1R, K to center st, P1, K to last st, M1L, K1. 2 sts inc.
Work Inc Row once, then every 2nd (4th, 6th, 2nd, 2nd, 4th, 4th, 10th, 6th) row 2 (5, 4, 2, 4, 2, 5, 2, 2) more times and then every 4th (6th, 8th, 4th, 4th, 6th, 0th, 0th, 8th) row 7 (2, 1, 4, 3, 2, 0, 0, 1) times. 10 (8, 6, 7, 8, 5, 6, 3, 4) sts inc at each edge. CO 20 (17, 13, 7, 8, 6, 6, 4, 5) sts at beginning of next 2 rows. Work the 5 sts at the edge of the sleeve in Seed st, and the rem sts in St st as established.
Work in established pattern for 2.75 (3, 3.5, 4.5, 5, 5.75, 6, 6.75, 7.25)" from sleeve CO edge, ending with a WS row before moving on to Lace Panel.

Neckline Shaping

AT THE SAME TIME, when piece measures 13.75 (15, 15.5, 16, 17, 17.75, 18.5, 19.25, 19.75)" from hem CO edge, begin V-neck decreases.
Neck Setup Row (RS): Work in pattern to center st, place P st on st holder, work to end of row.
Right and Left Fronts are worked at the same time. Attach a second ball of yarn for Left Front on next row.
Neck Dec Row (WS): Work in pattern to last 3 sts of Right Front, SSP, P1, drop Right Front yarn, with Left Front yarn P1, P2tog, work in pattern to end.
Neck Dec Row (RS): Work in pattern to last 3 sts in Left Front, K2tog, K1, drop Left Front yarn, with Right Front yarn K1, SSK, work in pattern to end.
Work a Neck Dec Row every row 17 (18, 20, 21, 26, 27, 29, 30, 30) times, then every other row 8 (8, 7, 7, 3, 3, 2, 2, 2) times. Once all V-neck decreases have been worked the stitch count at each sleeve should be 62 (63, 64, 65, 73, 74, 82, 83, 92) sts.

Lace Panel

When sleeves measure 2.75 (3, 3.5, 4.5, 5, 5.75, 6, 6.75, 7.25)" from sleeve CO edge, begin Lace Panel.
Dec Row (RS): Work 5 sts in Seed st, dec 8 (9, 10, 7, 11, 8, 12, 9, 10) sts evenly across Left Sleeve while working in St st, dec 8 (9, 10, 7, 11, 8, 12, 9, 10) sts evenly across Right Sleeve while working in St st to the last 5 sts, work in Seed st to end. 54 (54, 54, 58, 62, 66, 70, 74, 82) sts in each sleeve.
Next Row (WS): Work 5 sts in Seed St, P to last 5 sts of second sleeve, work 5 sts in Seed st.

Next Row (RS): Work 5 sts in Seed st, work German Honeycomb Lace pattern to last st of first sleeve, K1, K first st on second sleeve, work German Honeycomb Lace pattern to last 5 sts, work 5 sts in Seed st.

Work in established pattern with St st selvedge at neck edge until Lace measures 4 (4, 4, 4, 4.5, 4.5, 4.5, 4.5, 4.5)", ending with a Row 2 of German Honeycomb Lace pattern.

Back

Back Neck

Next Row (RS): Work 5 sts in Seed st, K to end of Left Sleeve, loosely CO 42 (44, 46, 46, 48, 50, 52, 52, 54) sts, K to last 5 sts of Right Sleeve, work 5 sts in Seed st. 150 (152, 154, 162, 172, 182, 192, 200, 218) sts total.

Work in established pattern (now on Row 4 of German Honeycomb Lace pattern) until Lace measures 2 (2, 2, 2.5, 2.5, 2.5, 2.5, 2.5)" from neck CO edge, or 6 (6, 6, 6, 7, 7, 7, 7, 7)" total, ending with a Row 3 or 6.

If ending with Row 3, work one more row in plain St st, maintaining first and last 5 sts in Seed st.

Back Sleeves

Inc Row (RS): Work 5 sts in Seed st, inc 25 (27, 29, 25, 33, 27, 35, 31, 31) sts evenly across center while working in St st to last 5 sts, work 5 sts in Seed st. 175 (179, 183, 187, 205, 209, 227, 231, 249) sts total.

Next Row (WS): Work 5 sts in Seed st, P82 (84, 86, 88, 97, 99, 108, 110, 119), K1, P to last 5 sts, work 5 sts in Seed st. Work in pattern as established with center st worked in rev St st, until sleeve measures 11.5 (12, 13, 15, 17, 18.25, 18.75, 20.5, 21.25)" total from sleeve CO edge, ending with a WS row.

BO 20 (17, 13, 7, 8, 6, 6, 4, 5) sts at the beg of the next 2 rows, maintaining center st in rev St st. 135 (145, 157, 173, 189, 197, 215, 223, 239) sts.

Dec Row (RS): K1, SSK, K to center st, P1, K to last 3 sts, K2tog, K1. 2 sts dec.

Work Dec Row once, then rep Dec Row every 4th (6th, 8th, 4th, 4th, 6th, 0th, 0th, 8th) row 7 (2, 1, 4, 3, 2, 0, 0, 1) times, and then every 2nd (4th, 6th, 2nd, 2nd, 4th, 4th, 10th, 6th) row 2 (5, 4, 2, 4, 2, 5, 2, 2) times. 10 (8, 6, 7, 8, 5, 6, 3, 4) sts dec at each edge. 115 (129, 145, 159, 173, 187, 203, 217, 231) sts total.

Body Increases

Using row markers will help while working this section.

Work one more WS row in established pattern.

Inc Row (RS): K1, M1R, K to center st, P1, K to last st, M1L, K1. 2 sts inc.

*Work an Inc Row, then work in St st, maintaining center rev St st for 2 (2, 2, 2, 2, 4, 4, 3)", ending with a WS row. Rep from * 4 (4, 0, 0, 0, 0, 2, 2, 3) more times. 10 (10, 2, 2, 2, 2, 6, 6, 8) sts inc.

Sizes 39.5, 43.5, 47, and 51" only:

**Work an Inc Row, and then work in St st, maintaining center rev St st, for 3", ending with a WS row. Rep from ** 2 more times. 6 sts inc.

125 (139, 153, 167, 181, 195, 209, 223, 239) sts total after all inc have been made.

Work in established pattern until piece measures 10 (11, 11, 11, 11, 11.5, 12, 12, 12)" from beg of body inc, ending with a WS row.

Hem

Selvedge Dec Row (RS): SSK, K to center st, P1, K to last 2 sts, K2tog. 2 sts dec. 123 (137, 151, 165, 179, 193, 207, 221, 237) sts total.

Next Row (WS): Work 5 sts in Seed st, P56 (63, 70, 77, 84, 91, 98, 105, 113), K1, P to last 5 sts, work 5 sts in Seed st.

Work in established pattern with 5 Seed sts at beg and end of row and center st in rev St st for 3", ending with a WS row. Switch to smaller needles and work in Seed st over all sts for 1", ending with a WS row.

BO all sts in pattern.

Finishing

Wash and block to measurements. Weave in ends.

Seam sleeve and side seams, leaving the bottom shirt-tail hems open where they transition to Seed st.

Neckband

Using smaller needles, and with RS facing, starting at center back neck, PU & K26 (26, 28, 28, 28, 30, 30, 32, 32), PM, PU & K1 st at back neck left corner, PU & K67 (67, 69, 69, 71, 71, 71, 73, 73) along V-neck side, PM, PU & P center V-neck st from holder, PU & K67 (67, 69, 69, 71, 71, 71, 73, 73) along V-neck side, PM, PU & K1 st at back neck right corner, PU & K25 (27, 27, 27, 29, 29, 29, 31, 31, 33) along back neck, PM for end of rnd. Join to work in the rnd. 188 (190, 196, 198, 202, 204, 206, 212, 214) sts total.

Rnd 1: *Work in Seed st to 1 sts before M, P2SP, removing M and placing it to the right of the st just made; rep from * twice more, work in Seed st to end of rnd. 6 sts dec.

Rnd 2: *Work in Seed st to M, SM, P1; rep from * twice more, work in Seed st to end of rnd.

Rep Rnds 1-2 twice more. Work Rnd 1 once more. 164 (166, 172, 174, 178, 180, 182, 188, 190) sts.

BO all sts in pattern.

Weave in ends.

A 15.5 (17.5, 19.75, 21.75, 23.5, 25.5, 27.75, 29.75, 31.5)"
B 17.25 (19.25, 21 23, 25, 27, 28.75, 30.75, 33)"
C 21 (22.25, 22.75, 22.5, 23.5, 24.75, 25.5, 26.25, 26.75)"
D 12 (13, 13, 13, 13, 13.5, 14, 14, 14)"
E 3.25 (3.25, 3.25, 2, 2, 2, 2, 2, 2)"
F 11.5 (12, 13, 15, 17, 18.25, 18.75, 20.5, 21.25)"
G 6 (6, 6, 6, 7, 7, 7, 7, 7)"
H 6.75 (7, 7.25, 7.25, 7.75, 8, 8.25, 8.25, 8.5)"
I 14 (15, 15, 15, 15, 15.5, 16, 16, 16)"
J 4.25 (3.5, 2.5, 2, 2.25, 1.5, 1.75, 1, 1.25)"

SIMPLE LACE TEE

by Sherrie Kibler

FINISHED MEASUREMENTS

36 (39, 42, 45, 48)" finished bust measurement; garment is meant to be worn with 4" of ease.

YARN

Knit Picks CotLin DK

(70% Tanguis Cotton, 30% Linen; 123 yards/50g): Raindrop 25326, 6 (6,7, 8,9) balls

NEEDLES

US 6 (4mm) circular needles, or size to obtain gauge

NOTIONS

Yarn Needle
Stitch Markers

GAUGE

16 sts and 26 rows = 4" in Lace pattern, blocked.

For pattern support, contact
Designs@Topazziknitting.com

Notes:
The two T-shaped pieces for this simple lace garment are worked flat and stitched together at the shoulders, under the arms, and along the sides to within a few inches of the bottom edge to create a longer, loose-fitting garment. Seed stitch is used as a border along the boat neckline, sleeve edges, slit, and bottom edge.

A circular needle is used to accommodate the large number of stitches.

Seed Stitch (worked flat over an even number of sts)
Row 1 (WS): (K1, P1) to end.
Row 2 (RS): (P1, K1) to end.
Rep Rows 1-2 for pattern.

Lace Pattern (worked over a multiple of 6 sts plus 2 selvage sts)
Row 1 (RS): K1, *K3, YO, CDD, YO, repeat from * until last st, K1.
Row 2 (WS): P.
Row 3: K1, *YO, CDD, YO, K3, repeat from * until last st, K1.
Row 4: P.
Rep Rows 1-4 for pattern.

DIRECTIONS

Back
CO 76 (82, 88, 94, 100) sts. Do not join. Work 5 rows in Seed st.
Next Row (RS): (P1, K1) twice, PM, (P1, K1) to last 4 sts, PM, (P1, K1) twice.
Next Row: (K1, P1) twice, SM, P to M, SM, (K1, P1) twice.

Bottom With Side Slits
Row 1 (RS): (P1, K1) twice, SM, work Lace Pattern Row 1 to M, SM, (P1, K1) twice.
Row 2 (WS): (K1, P1) twice, SM, work Lace Pattern Row 2 to M, SM, (K1, P1) twice.
Row 3: (P1, K1) twice, SM, work Lace Pattern Row 3 to M, SM, (P1, K1) twice.
Row 4: (K1, P1) twice, SM, work Lace Pattern Row 4 to M, SM, (K1, P1) twice.
Work 4 (4, 5, 5, 5) additional repeats of Rows 1-4 then work Rows 1-3 once more.

Body
Next Row (WS): (K1, PFB) twice, remove M, P to M, remove M, (K1, PFB) twice. 80 (86, 92, 98, 104) sts.
Work Lace Pattern until piece measures approximately 14 (14, 15, 16, 16)" from CO edge, ending with Row 4.

Sleeve
Next Row (RS): Use Backward Loop CO to CO 22 (22, 22, 28, 28), (P1, K1) twice, K18 (18, 18, 24, 24), work Lace Pattern Row 1 to end of row. 102 (108, 114, 126, 132) sts.
Next Row (WS): Use Backward Loop CO to CO 22 (22, 22, 28, 28), (K1, P1) twice, P18 (18, 18, 24, 24), work Lace Pattern Row 2 to last 4 sts, PM, (K1, P1) twice. 124 (130, 136, 154, 160) sts.
Next Row: (P1, K1) twice, PM, work Lace Pattern Row 3 to M, SM, (P1, K1) twice.
Next Row: (K1, P1) twice, SM, work Lace Pattern Row 4 to M, SM, (K1, P1) twice.

Work the following 4 rows until sleeve measures 7.25 (7.25, 8.25, 8.25, 9.25)" from sleeve CO, ending on an even row:
Row 1: (P1, K1) twice, SM, work Lace Pattern Row 1 to M, SM, (P1, K1) twice.
Row 2: (K1, P1) twice, SM, work Lace Pattern Row 2 to M, SM, (K1, P1) twice.
Row 3: (P1, K1) twice, SM, work Lace Pattern Row 3 to M, SM, (P1, K1) twice.
Row 4: (K1, P1) twice, SM, work Lace Pattern Row 4 to M, SM, (K1, P1) twice.

Work 5 rows of Seed Stitch pattern, BO in pattern loosely with WS facing.

Front
Work same as Back.

Finishing
Weave in ends, wash and block pieces to diagram. Join the front and back pieces by sewing 10 (10.75, 11, 12.75, 13.5)" shoulder seams each side, leaving center 11 (11, 12, 13, 13)" unsewn for neck opening. Beginning 1" below the top of Seed Stitch slit trim, sew side and underarm seams.

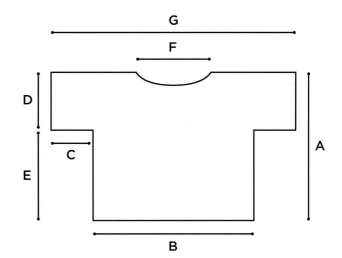

A 22 (22, 24, 25, 26)"
B 19.5 (21, 22.5, 24, 25.5)"
C 5.5 (5.5, 5.5, 7, 7)"
D 8 (8, 9, 9, 10)"
E 14 (14, 15, 16, 16)"
F 11 (11, 12, 13, 13)"
G 31 (32.5, 34, 38.5, 40)"

SIMPLY SURPRISED TEE

by Ivy Sipes

FINISHED MEASUREMENTS

32(35.75, 40, 43.75, 48, 51.75, 56, 59.75, 64)" finished bust measurement; garment is meant to be worn with 4" of ease

YARN

Knit Picks Curio
(100% Cotton; 721 yards/100g): Natural 26254, Sagebrush 26267, 2(2, 2, 2, 2, 2, 3, 3, 3) balls each

NEEDLES

US 3 (3.25 mm) straight or 24" or longer circular needles, or size to obtain gauge

NOTIONS

Yarn Needle
Stitch Markers
Stitch Holders or spare needle

GAUGE

26 sts and 35 rows = 4" in St st with yarn held double, blocked
21 sts and 28 rows= 4" in Lace Back Stitch with yarn held double, blocked.

Notes:

The Simply Surprised Tee is knit in pieces from the bottom up then seamed. The front is knit in stockinette with waist decreasing for a flattering loose fitting tee. The back has an easy lace panel which will add some fun while knitting and especially wearing! The yarn is held doubled, with one strand of each color throughout to create a marled effect.

Garter Stitch (worked flat)
Row 1: K to end
Rep Row 1 for patt.

Stockinette Stitch (worked flat)
Row1 (WS): P to end.
Row 2 (RS): K to end.
Rep Rows 1-2 for patt.

Lace Back Stitch (worked flat)
After every 8 row pattern repeat, another multiple will be repeated to each side of the center stitch. A removable marker can be used to keep track of the center st.
Row 1 (RS): K2tog, PM, K2, YO, K1, YO, K2, PM, SSK.
Row 2 and All WS Rows: P.
Row 3: K2tog, SM, K2, YO, K1, YO, K2, SM, SSK,
Row 5: K2tog, SM, K2, YO, K1, YO, CDD, YO, K1, YO, K2, SM, SSK
Row 7: K2tog, SM, K2, YO, K1, YO, K3, YO, K1, YO, K2, SM, SSK.
Row 9: K2tog, K2, YO, (K1, YO, K3tog, YO) rep to center st, K1, (YO, Sl1, K2tog, PSSO, YO, K1) rep to 2 sts before M, YO, K2, SSK.
Row 11: K2tog, K2, YO, (K1, YO, K3tog, YO) rep to 1 st before center st, K3, (YO, Sl1, K2tog, PSSO, YO, K1) rep to 2 sts before M, YO, K2, SSK.
Row 13: K2tog, K2, YO, (K1, YO, K3tog, YO) rep to 2 sts before center st, K1, YO, CDD, YO, K1, (YO, Sl1, K2tog, PSSO, YO, K1) rep to 2 sts before M, YO, K2, SSK.
Row 15: K2tog, K2, YO, (K1, YO, K3tog, YO) rep to 3 sts before center st, K2, YO, CDD, YO, K2, (YO, Sl1, K2tog, PSSO, YO, K1) rep to 2 sts before M, YO, K2, SSK.

If working from the chart, read the charts RS rows (odd numbers) from right to left, and WS rows (even numbers) from left to right.

Three Needle Bind-Off
Start with right sides together and the same amount of stitches on each needle. Holding the needles parallel, insert a third needle into the first stitch on each parallel needle, knitting them together. Repeat for the second stitch. *Pass the first stitch over the second stitch on the right needle. Insert right needle into next stitch on both needles knitting them together repeat from *until one stitch remains.

DIRECTIONS

Front
This sweater has both RS and WS shaping. Uses the appropriate Decrease or Increase row as needed.

Holding one strand of each color, loosely CO 120(126, 136, 148, 162, 174, 188, 198, 210) sts.

Work in Garter st for 10 rows.

Work in St st for 4 (5, 7, 7, 7, 7, 9, 12) rows.

Work on Dec Row, using appropriate Dec Row instructions.
Dec Row(RS): K1, K2tog, K to 3 sts before end, SSK, K1.
Dec Row (WS): P1, P2tog TBL, P to 3 sts before end, P2tog, P1.

Rep Dec Row every 4 (6, 8, 8, 8, 8, 8, 9, 10) rows 10 (7, 5, 5, 5, 5, 4, 3) more times, until 98 (110, 124, 136, 150, 162, 176, 188, 202) sts remain.

Continue working in St st until piece measures 7" or desired length from CO ending on a WS row.

Work one Inc Row, using appropriate Inc Row instructions.
Inc Row (RS): K1, M1, K to last stitch, M1, K1.
Inc Row (WS): P1, M1, P to last st, M1, P1.

Rep Inc Row every 25 (26, 25, 24, 24, 23, 22, 21, 20) rows 2 more times until 104 (116, 130, 142, 156, 168, 182, 194, 208) sts remain.

Work in St st until piece measures 22.5 (23, 23.25, 23.5, 23.75, 24, 24, 24.5, 24.5)" or desired length ending on a WS row.

Neck
Next Row (RS): K 23 (27, 33, 37, 42, 47, 52, 57, 62) sts, BO 58(62, 64, 68, 72, 74, 78, 80, 84) sts, K to end. 46 (54, 66, 74, 84, 94, 104, 114, 124)sts remain, 23 (27, 33, 37, 42, 47, 52, 57, 62)sts each shoulder.

Place sts on holder or spare needle.

Back
Work same as Front until piece measures 15.75 (16.25, 16, 16, 16, 15.5, 15.5, 15.5)" or desired length ending on WS.

Inc Row: K52 (58, 65, 71, 78, 84, 91, 97, 104), M1, K52 (58, 65, 71, 78, 84, 91, 97, 104). 105 (117, 131, 143, 157, 169, 183, 195, 209) sts.

Next Row: P.

Lace Back Pattern
Row 1 (RS): K48 (54, 61, 67, 74, 80, 87, 93, 100), work row 1 of Lace Back Stitch from chart or written instructions, K48 (54, 61, 67, 74, 80, 87, 93, 100). 105 (117, 131, 143, 157, 169, 183, 195, 209) sts total.
Row 2 and All WS Rows: P.
Row 3 and All RS Rows: K to 2 sts before M, work Lace Back Stitch, K to end.

Work through row 16, then rep Lace Back Stitch rows 9-16, working another multiple every repeat, until piece measures 22.5 (23, 23.25, 23.5, 23.75, 24, 24, 24.5, 24.5)" or desired length ending on a WS row.

Work in St sts for 2 rows.

Next Row: K 23 (27, 33, 37, 42, 47, 52, 57, 62) sts, BO 59 (63, 65, 69, 73, 75, 79, 81, 85) sts, K to end of row. 46 (54, 66, 74, 84, 94, 104, 114, 124) sts remain, 23 (27, 33, 37, 42, 47, 52, 57, 62) sts each shoulder.

Shoulders

With right sides together, using Three Needle Bind Off, BO front and back pieces together.

Sleeves (make 2)

The Sleeves are worked by picking up sts at under arm and working in Garter st.

Starting at 16 (16, 15.75, 15.5, 15.25, 15, 14.5, 14.5, 14)" or desired length from CO edge, PU & K 85 (91, 98, 104, 111, 117, 124, 130, 137) sts along armhole of front and back.

Knit Garter st for 6 rows.

BO in pattern.

Finishing

Wash and block to diagram, seam underarms and sides. Weave in ends.

Lace Back Stitch Chart

Legend codes used in the table below: (blank) = knit · O = yo · / = k2tog · \ = ssk · k3tog · spso = sl1 k2tog psso · CDD = Central Double Dec · ▓ = no stitch / shaded

23	22	21	20	19	18	17	16	15	14	13	12	11	10	9	8	7	6	5	4	3	2	1	Row
																							16
\			O		O	spso	O			O	CDD	O			O	/	O		O			/	15
▓																							14
	\			O		O	spso	O		O	CDD	O		O	/	O		O		/			13
▓	▓																						12
		\			O		O	spso	O				O	/	O		O			/			11
▓	▓	▓																					10
			\			O		O	spso	O		O	/	O		O			/				9
▓	▓	▓	▓																				8
				\			O		O			O		O				/					7
▓	▓	▓	▓	▓														▓	▓	▓	▓	▓	6
					\			O	CDD	O		O				/	▓	▓	▓	▓	▓	▓	5
▓	▓	▓	▓	▓											▓	▓	▓	▓	▓	▓	▓	▓	4
						\			O			O			/	▓	▓	▓	▓	▓	▓	▓	3
▓	▓	▓	▓	▓	▓							▓	▓	▓	▓	▓	▓	▓	▓	▓	▓	▓	2
					\				O		O		/	▓	▓	▓	▓	▓	▓	▓	▓	▓	1

Legend

knit
RS: knit stitch
WS: purl stitch

O — yo
Yarn Over

⟋ — k2tog
Knit two stitches together as one stitch

⟍ — ssk
Slip one stitch as if to knit. Slip another stitch as if to knit. Insert left-hand needle into front of these two stitches and knit them together.

k3 tog
Knit three stitches together as one

sl1 k2tog psso
slip 1, k2tog, pass slip stitch over, k2tog

Central Double Dec
Slip first and second stitches together as if to knit. Knit one stitch. Pass two slipped stitches over the knit stitch.

Left Side Repeat

Right Side Repeat

Place Marker

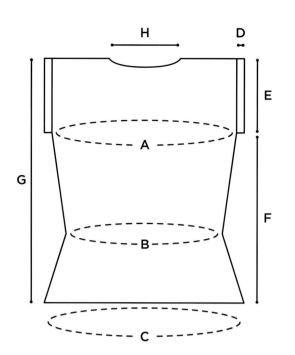

A 32 (35.75, 40, 43.75, 48, 51.75, 56, 59.75, 64)"
B 30.25 (33.75, 38.25, 41.75, 46.25, 49.75, 54.25, 57.75, 62.25)"
C 37 (38.75, 41.75, 45.5, 49.75, 53.5, 57.75, 61, 64.5)"
D .5 (.5, .5, .5, .5, .5, .5, .5, .5)"
E 6.5 (7, 7.5, 8, 8.5, 9, 9.5, 10, 10.5)"
F 16 (16, 15.75, 15.5, 15.25, 15, 14.5, 14.5, 14)"
G 22.5 (23, 23.25, 23.5, 23.75, 24, 24, 24.5, 24.5)"
H 9 (9.5, 9.75, 10.5, 11, 11.5, 12, 12.25, 13)"

SPROUTS TEE

by Nadya Stallings

FINISHED MEASUREMENTS

35 (39.25, 43, 46.5, 51, 54.5, 59.75, 65.5)" finished bust measurement; garment is meant to be worn with 2.5-5" of ease depending on size

YARN

Knit Picks Shine Sport
(60% Pima Cotton, 40% Modal® natural beech wood fiber; 110 yards/50g): Platinum 25338, 6 (7, 8, 9, 10, 12, 13, 14) balls

NEEDLES

US 4 (3.5mm) 32" or longer circular needles, or size to obtain gauge

NOTIONS

Yarn Needle
Stitch Markers
Scrap yarn or stitch holder
Row counters

GAUGE

22 sts and 28 rows = 4" over Rib Stitch pattern, gently blocked

For pattern support, contact
nadyasdesigns@gmail.com

Notes:

Sprouts Tee is worked from bottom up in the round slightly widening towards armholes. Then the front and back are worked flat. A few stitches for short "kimono" sleeves are picked up and further worked along with each body panel with sleeve and shoulder shaping. Neckline is rounded at front and shaped with short rows. This design also features a lace motif worked asymmetrically on one side of the front.

Rib Stitch Pattern (worked flat over multiples of 9 plus 4 sts)
Row 1: K1, *P2, K7, rep from *, P2, K1
Row 2: P1, *K2, P7, rep from *, K2, P1.

M1: CO 1 st with Loop CO method. For a tutorial, please see http://tutorials.knitpicks.com/loop-cast-on/

Sewn Bind-off
Cut the working yarn to about 3 times as long as your finished piece of knitting. Thread yarn onto blunt needle. *Pass the yarn needle through the first two sts from right to left. Pass the yarn needle through the first st on the knitting needle from left to right. Drop the first st off the knitting needle. Repeat from * until one st remains. Sew through this last st from right to left.

When working chart flat, read the chart RS rows (odd numbers) from right to left, and WS rows (even numbers) from left to right.
When working chart in the rnd, follow all chart rows from right to left, reading them as RS rows.
When working shaping, refer to shaping diagram when necessary.

DIRECTIONS

Body
The body is worked bottom-up in the rnd to the armholes.
CO 172 (196, 216, 236, 260, 280, 312, 348) sts. PM (left side) and join to work in the round, being careful not to twist sts.
Rnd 1: P.
Rnd 2: K.
Rnds 3 and 4: *K0 (0, 0, 0, 1, 0, 0, 0) P0 (0, 1, 0, 2, 0, 0, 0), K6 (3, 7, 4, 7, 6, 5, 5), [P2, K7] 8 (10, 10, 12, 12, 14, 16, 18) times, P2, K6 (3, 7, 4, 7, 6, 5, 5), P0 (0, 1, 0, 2, 0, 0, 0), K0 (0, 0, 0, 1, 0, 0, 0)*, PM (right side), rep from * to * once.
Rnd 5: K0 (0, 0, 0, 1, 0, 0, 0), P0 (0, 1, 0, 2, 0, 0, 0), K6 (3, 7, 4, 7, 6, 5, 5), *P2, K7; rep from * 1 (2, 2, 3, 3, 4, 5, 6) time(s), work 27 sts from Lace Chart 1, work as established to end of the rnd.
Work in pattern as established for 13 (13, 13, 15, 15, 17, 21, 29) more rnds.
Inc Rnd: Work 1 st, M1, work in pattern to 1 st before next M, M1, work 1 st, SM, work 1 st, M1, work in pattern to 1 st before M, M1, work 1 st, SM. 4 sts inc.
Incorporating increased sts into Rib Stitch pattern within the markers, rep Inc Rnd every 14th (14th, 14th, 16th, 16th, 18th, 22nd, 0th) rnd 4 (4, 4, 3, 3, 2, 2, 0) more times and then every 0th (0th, 0th, 14th, 14th, 16th, 20th, 28th) rnd 0 (0, 0, 1, 1, 2, 1, 2) more times. 192 (216, 236, 256, 280, 300, 328, 360) sts.
Work as established for 1 more rnd.

Next Rnd: Work 96 (108, 118, 128, 140, 150, 164, 180) Front sts to right side marker and then place them on hold. The remaining 96 (108, 118, 128, 140, 150, 164, 180) sts will be worked for the Back.

Back
The Back is worked flat along with the short sleeves.

Sleeve Shaping
Beginning with a RS Row, work established Rib Stitch pattern for 2 rows.
Inc Row (RS): With Cable CO technique CO 4 sts; incorporating CO sts into established Rib Stitch pattern, cont to end of the row; with Backward Loop CO technique CO 4 sts. 104 (116, 126, 136, 148, 158, 172, 188) sts.
Next Row (WS): Work as established, incorporating new CO sts into Rib Stitch pattern.

Cuff Slope Shaping
Inc Row (RS): K1, M1, work in pattern to last st, M1, K1. 2 sts inc. Rep Inc Row every 10th (8th, 6th, 4th, 4th, 4th, 4th, 4th) row 1 (3, 2, 11, 10, 9, 9, 7) more times and then every 8th (6th, 4th, 2nd, 2nd, 2nd, 2nd, 2nd) row 3 (2, 8, 5, 10, 13, 14, 21) more times, ending with WS row. 114 (128, 148, 170, 190, 204, 220, 246) sts.
Work as established for 8 (6, 4, 2, 2, 2, 2) more rows.

Sleeve Slope Shaping
BO 2 (2, 3, 4, 8, 9, 10, 18) sts at beginning of next 2 rows 8 (9, 7, 2, 2, 2, 2) times and then BO 3 (3, 4, 5, 9, 10, 11, 19) sts at beginning of next 2 rows 1 (2, 3, 7, 4, 4, 4, 2) more time(s). 76 (80, 82, 84, 86, 88, 92, 98) sts.

Shoulders Shaping
Next Row (RS): BO 19 (19, 19, 19, 19, 19, 20, 22) right shoulder sts, work as established to end of the row.
Next Row (WS): BO 19 (19, 19, 19, 19, 19, 20, 22) left shoulder sts, place remaining 38 (42, 44, 46, 48, 50, 52, 54) neck sts on st holder.

Front
Front is worked flat along with short sleeves. Return Front sts to needles ready to work a RS row.
Please read through the entire Front instructions before beginning. Begin with the Sleeve CO section. Then the Cuff Slope Shaping and Neckline Shaping happen simultaneously and during the shaping, the Lace Pattern will change from Chart 1 to Chart 2.
When Rnds/Rows 1-8 of Lace Chart 1 has been worked 10 (11, 12, 13, 14, 14, 15, 15) times total, then begin working from Lace Chart 2.
When Rows 1-24 of Lace Chart 2 are complete, continue in Rib Stitch pattern until all shaping is completed.

Sleeve CO
Beginning with a RS Row, work in established, Lace and Rib Stitch patterns for 2 rows.

Inc Row (RS): With Cable CO technique CO 4 sts, incorporating CO sts into established stitch pattern, cont to end of the row, with Backward Loop CO technique CO 4 sts. 104 (116, 126, 136, 148, 158, 172, 188) sts.

Next Row (WS): Work in pattern as established, incorporating new CO sts.

Cuff Slope Shaping and Sleeve Slope Shaping

Work Inc Row Cuff Slope Shaping (same as Back) for 40 (44, 48, 54, 54, 56, 58, 60) rows then begin Neckline Shaping. Once Neckline Shaping begins, work appropriate Right/Left Side Inc Row instead of Inc Row until Cuff Slope Shaping is complete.

Neckline Shaping

At this point Neckline Shaping is worked with short rows. The Cuff Slope/Sleeve Slope shapings continue as for Back but for one Front side at a time, at the beginning of the rows for Left Front and at the end of the rows for Right Front.

Left Front Inc Row (RS): K1, M1, work in pattern according to Neckline Shaping instruction.

Left Side Neckline Shaping

PM on each side of center 10 (10, 12, 12, 12, 14, 14, 14) sts.

Short Row 1 (RS) and all RS Short Rows, unless otherwise instructed: Work in pattern to next M, remove M, W&T.

Short Row 2 (WS): Work in pattern for 2 (3, 3, 3, 4, 4, 4, 5) sts, PM, cont in pattern to end of row.

Short Row 4: Work in pattern for 2 (3, 3, 3, 3, 3, 4, 4) sts, PM, cont in pattern to end of row.

Short Row 6: Work in pattern for 2 (2, 2, 3, 3, 3, 3, 3) sts, PM, cont in pattern to end of row.

Short Row 8 & 10: Work in pattern for 2 sts, PM, cont in pattern to end of row.

Short Rows 12, 14, 16 & 18: Work in pattern for 1 st, PM, cont in pattern to end of row.

Short Row 20: Work in pattern.

Begin Right Side Neckline Shaping and continue Cuff Slope Shaping and Sleeve Slope Shaping, but Inc Row is worked as follows:

Right Side Inc Row (RS): Work in pattern according to Neckline Shaping instruction to last st, M1, K1.

Right Side Neckline Shaping

Short Row 21 (RS): Work in pattern to end of row, working wrapped sts tog with wraps.

Short Row 22 (WS) and all WS Short Rows, unless otherwise instructed: Work in pattern to next M, remove M, W&T.

Short Row 23 (RS): Work in pattern for 2 (3, 3, 3, 4, 4, 4, 5) sts, PM, cont in pattern to end of row.

Short Row 25: Work in pattern for 2 (3, 3, 3, 3, 3, 4, 4) sts, PM, cont in pattern to end of row.

Short Row 27: Work in pattern for 2 (2, 2, 3, 3, 3, 3, 3) sts, PM, cont in pattern to end of row.

Short Row 29 & 31: Work in pattern for 2 sts, PM, cont in pattern to end of row.

Short Rows 33, 35, 37 & 39: Work in pattern for 1 st, PM, cont in pattern to end of row.

Short Row 40 (RS): Work in pattern to end of row, working wrapped sts tog with wraps.

Sleeve Slope Shaping
At the same time when Cuff Slope for either Right or Left Front is completed, work Sleeve Slope Shaping:

Front Left
BO 2 (2, 3, 4, 8, 9, 10, 18) sts at beginning of next RS row 8 (9, 7, 2, 2, 2, 2, 2) times and then BO 3 (3, 4, 5, 9, 10, 11, 19) sts at beginning of next RS row 1 (2, 3, 7, 4, 4, 4, 2) more times.

Front Right
BO 2 (2, 3, 4, 8, 9, 10, 18) sts at beginning of next WS row 8 (9, 7, 2, 2, 2, 2, 2) times and then BO 3 (3, 4, 5, 9, 10, 11, 19) sts at beginning of next WS row 1 (2, 3, 7, 4, 4, 4, 2) more times. Cont in pattern until all slope and neck shapings are completed.

Shoulders Shaping
Next Row (RS): BO 19 (19, 19, 19, 19, 19, 20, 22) right shoulder sts, cont in pattern to end of the row.
Next Row (WS): BO 19 (19, 19, 19, 19, 19, 20, 22) left shoulder sts, place remaining 38 (42, 44, 46, 48, 50, 52, 54) neck sts on st holder.

Finishing
Sew underarms, sleeve sides and shoulders.

Neck Band
With RS facing and beginning at the back center, place all 76 (84, 88, 92, 96, 100, 104, 108) live neck sts on working needle and join to work in the rnd.
Rnd 1: P.
Rnd 2: K.
Rep Rnd 1 one more time.
BO with Sewn BO technique or stretchy BO method of your preference.

Cuff Trims
With RS facing and beginning at the underarm point PU & K 33 (33, 38, 44, 48, 50, 51, 56) sts up to the shoulder seam, PU and K 33 (33, 38, 44, 48, 50, 51, 56) sts down from the shoulder, join to work in the rnd. 66 (66, 76, 88, 96, 100, 102, 112) sts.

Rnd 1: P
Rnd 2: K
BO with Sewn BO technique or stretchy BO method of your preference.

Weave in ends, wash and block to diagram.

Shaping Diagram

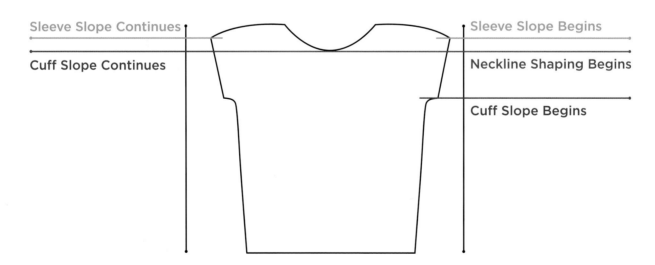

Lace Chart 1 (Flat)

	27	26	25	24	23	22	21	20	19	18	17	16	15	14	13	12	11	10	9	8	7	6	5	4	3	2	1	
8								●	●								●	●								●	●	
			O	Λ	O			●	●			O	Λ	O			●	●			O	Λ	O			●	●	7
6								●	●								●	●								●	●	
		O	/		\	O		●	●		O	/		\	O		●	●		O	/		\	O		●	●	5
4								●	●								●	●								●	●	
	\	O			O	/		●	●	\	O			O	/		●	●	\	O				O	/	●	●	3
2								●	●								●	●								●	●	
	\		O		O		/	●	●	\		O		O		/	●	●	\		O		O		/	●	●	1

Lace Chart 1 (In the Round)

27	26	25	24	23	22	21	20	19	18	17	16	15	14	13	12	11	10	9	8	7	6	5	4	3	2	1	
								●	●								●	●								●	●	8
		O	Λ	O			●	●			O	Λ	O			●	●			O	Λ	O			●	●		7
								●	●								●	●								●	●	6
	O	/		\	O		●	●		O	/		\	O		●	●		O	/		\	O		●	●		5
								●	●								●	●								●	●	4
\	O			O	/		●	●	\	O			O	/		●	●	\	O				O	/	●	●		3
								●	●								●	●								●	●	2
\		O		O		/	●	●	\		O		O		/	●	●	\		O		O		/	●	●		1

Legend

knit
RS: knit stitch
WS: purl stitch

purl
RS: purl stitch
WS: knit stitch

yo
Yarn Over

k2tog
Knit two stitches together as one stitch

ssk
Slip one stitch as if to knit. Slip another stitch as if to knit. Insert left-hand needle into front of these two stitches and knit them together.

Central Double Dec
Slip first and second stitches together as if to knit. Knit one stitch. Pass two slipped stitches over the knit stitch.

M1
Cast on one stitch with Loop cast on method.

Slip
Slip stitch as if to knit, holding yarn in back.

Pattern Repeat

Lace Chart 2

	27	26	25	24	23	22	21	20	19	18	17	16	15	14	13	12	11	10	9	8	7	6	5	4	3	2	1	
24								•	•								•	•								•	•	
				S				•	•								•	•								•	•	23
22								•	•								•	•								•	•	
			M	∧	M			•	•								•	•								•	•	21
20								•	•								•	•								•	•	
		M	/			\	M	•	•								•	•								•	•	19
18								•	•								•	•								•	•	
	M	/				\	M	•	•								•	•								•	•	17
16								•	•								•	•								•	•	
			O	∧	O			•	•				S				•	•								•	•	15
14								•	•								•	•								•	•	
		O	/			\	O	•	•		M	∧	M				•	•								•	•	13
12								•	•								•	•								•	•	
	\	O				O	/	•	•		M	/		\	M		•	•								•	•	11
10								•	•								•	•								•	•	
	\		O		O		/	•	•	M	/			\	M		•	•								•	•	9
8								•	•								•	•								•	•	
			O	∧	O			•	•			O	∧	O			•	•				S				•	•	7
6								•	•								•	•								•	•	
		O	/			\	O	•	•			O	/		\	O	•	•			M	∧	M			•	•	5
4								•	•								•	•								•	•	
		\	O			O	/	•	•	\		O			O	/	•	•		M	/		\	M		•	•	3
2								•	•								•	•								•	•	
		\	O		O		/	•	•	\		O		O		/	•	•	M	/			\		M	•	•	1

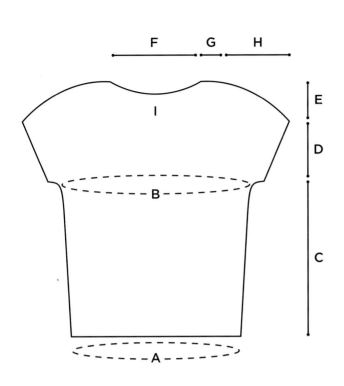

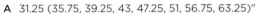

A 31.25 (35.75, 39.25, 43, 47.25, 51, 56.75, 63.25)"
B 35 (39.25, 43, 46.5, 51, 54.5, 59.75, 65.5)"
C 10.75 (10.75, 10.75, 12, 12, 13.25, 13.25, 13.25)"
D 6.75 (6.75, 7.5, 8.75, 9.5, 9.75, 10.25, 11)"
E 2.75 (3.5, 3.25, 2.75, 2, 2, 2, 1.5)"
F 7 (7.75, 8, 8.25, 8.75, 9, 9.5, 9.75)"
G 3.5 (3.5, 3.5, 3.5, 3.5, 3.5, 3.75, 4)"
H 7 (7.75, 9.5, 11.25, 13, 14, 15.25, 17.5)"
I 3.25 (3.25, 3.25, 3.25, 3.25, 3.25, 3.25, 3.25)"

TEGAN TEE

by Sue Gleave

FINISHED MEASUREMENTS

34 (38.25, 42.25, 46.25, 50.25, 54.25, 58.5, 62.5, 66.5)" finished bust measurement; garment is meant to be worn with 2" of ease

YARN

Knit Picks Lindy Chain
(70% Linen, 30% Pima Cotton; 180 yards/50g): Tumeric 27003, 4 (4, 5, 6, 6, 7, 7, 7, 7) balls

NEEDLES

US 4 (3.5mm) 24"circular needle, or size to obtain gauge

NOTIONS

Yarn Needle
Stitch Markers
Scrap yarn or stitch holder

GAUGE

21 sts and 28 rnds = 4" over Milanese Lace Pattern in the rnd, blocked
22 sts and 28 rows = 4" in St st, blocked

For pattern support, contact
sue@nativeyarns.co.uk

Notes:

Inspired by the patterns made by sunlight dancing on the surface of the sea, this is a tee to celebrate the return of warmer weather and the expectation of long summer days and of sea and sand.

The Tegan Tee is an elegant top with lace panels incorporated into the side. It has a gentle A-line shape, with decreases made at the border of the stockinette and lace sections. It's worked from the bottom up, in the round until divided for the armholes. The front and back are then worked flat. The top is seamed at the shoulders and finished with a seed stitch neckband, worked in the round.

RH Milanese Lace (in the rnd, over multiples of 6 plus 2 sts)
Rnd 1: K1, *K4, K2tog, YO; repeat from * to last st, K1.
Rnd 2: K1, *K3, K2tog, K1, YO; repeat from * to last st, K1.
Rnd 3: K1, *K2, K2tog, K2, YO; repeat from * to last st, K1.
Rnd 4: K1, *K1, K2tog, K3, YO; repeat from * to last st, K1.
Rnd 5: K1, *K2tog, K4, YO; repeat from * to last st, K1.
Rnd 6: *K2tog, YO, K4; repeat from * to last 2 sts, K2.
Rnd 7: K1, *K1, YO, K3, K2tog; repeat from * to last st, K1.
Rnd 8: K1, *K2, YO, K2, K2tog; repeat from * to last st, K1.
Rnd 9: K1, *K3, YO, K1, K2tog; repeat from * to last st, K1.
Rnd 10: K1, *K4, YO, K2tog; repeat from * to last st, K1.
Rep Rnds 1-10 for pattern.

LH Milanese Lace (in the rnd, over multiples of 6 plus 2 sts)
Rnd 1: K1, *YO, SKP, K4; repeat from * to last st, K1.
Rnd 2: K1, *YO, K1, SKP, K3; repeat from * to last st, K1.
Rnd 3: K1, *YO, K2, SKP, K2; repeat from * to last st, K1.
Rnd 4: K1, *YO, K3, SKP, K1; repeat from * to last st, K1.
Rnd 5: K1, *YO, K4, SKP; repeat from * to last st, K1.
Rnd 6: K2, *K4, YO, SKP; repeat from * to end of row.
Rnd 7: K1, *SKP, K3, YO, K1; repeat from * to last st, K1.
Rnd 8: K1, *SKP, K2, YO, K2; repeat from * to last st, K1.
Rnd 9: K1, *SKP, K1, YO, K3; repeat from * to last st, K1.
Rnd 10: K1, *SKP, YO, K4; repeat from * to last st, K1.
Rep Rnds 1-10 for pattern.

If using the charts, read all rows as RS rows from right to left.

Seed St (in the rnd over an even number of sts)
Rnd1: *K1, P1; repeat from * to end of rnd.
Rnd 2: *P1, K1; repeat from * to end of rnd.
Rep Rnds 1-2 for pattern.

DIRECTIONS

Body
CO 196, (218, 240, 262, 284, 306, 328, 350, 372) sts, PM, and join to work in the rnd, taking care not to twist the stitches.
Rnd 1: K60 (65, 76, 81, 92, 103, 108, 119, 130) sts across the back, PM, work LH Milanese Lace for 38 (44, ,44, 50, 50, 50, 56, 56, 56) sts, PM, K60 (65, 76, 81, 92, 103, 108, 119, 130) sts across the front, PM, work RH Milanese Lace for 38 (44, ,44, 50, 50, 50, 56, 56, 56) sts, SM.
Rep Rnd 1 39 times.

Dec Rnd: K2tog, K to 2 sts before M, SKP, SM, work LH Milanese Lace to M, SM, K2tog, K to 2 sts before M, SKP, SM, work RH Milanese Lace to M, SM. 4 sts dec.
Maintaining St st and Lace sections, rep Dec Rnd every 20th rnd 2 more times. 184 (206, 228, 250, 272, 294, 316, 338, 360) sts.
Work 39 (39, 39, 39, 39, 34, 34, 34, 34) rnds in pattern.

Separate Front & Back
Next Rnd: Starting with the end of rnd M, remove Ms as you come to them. K173, (192, 214, 235, 257, 279, 300, 324, 348) sts.
Next Rnd: K76, (87, 98, 105, 116, 127, 134, 141, 148) BO 16 (16, 16, 20, 20, 20, 24, 28, 32), K76, (87, 98, 105, 116, 127, 134, 141, 148) BO 16 (16, 16, 20, 20, 20, 24, 28, 32).

Back
The Front & Back are now separated. Place the stitches of the Front on a st holder.
Row 1 (RS): BO 3 (3, 4, 4, 4, 4, 5, 6, 6) sts, K to end. 73 (84, 94, 101, 112, 123, 129, 135, 142) sts.
Row 2 (WS): BO 3 (3, 4, 4, 4, 4, 5, 6, 6) sts, P to end. 70 (81, 90, 97, 108, 119, 124, 129, 136) sts.
Row 3: BO 2 (3, 3, 3, 3, 4, 5, 6, 6) sts, K to end. 68 (78, 87, 94, 105, 115, 119, 123, 130) sts.
Row 4: BO 2 (3, 3, 3, 3, 4, 5, 6, 6) sts, P to end. 66 (75, 84, 91, 102, 111, 114, 117, 124) sts.
Row 5: BO 1 (2, 2, 3, 3, 4, 4, 5, 5) sts, K to end. 65 (73, 82, 88, 99, 107, 110, 112, 119) sts.
Row 6: BO 1 (2, 2, 3, 3, 4, 4, 5, 5) sts, P to end. 64 (71, 80, 85, 96, 103, 106, 107, 114) sts.
Row 7: BO 1 (1, 1, 2, 2, 3, 3, 2, 3) sts, K to end. 63 (70, 79, 83, 94, 100, 103, 105, 111) sts.
Row 8: BO 1 (1, 1, 2, 2, 3, 3, 2, 3) sts, P to end. 62 (69, 78, 81, 92, 97, 100, 103, 108) sts.
Row 9: BO 0 (0, 0, 0, 0, 0, 0, 1, 2) sts, K to end. 62 (69, 78, 81, 92, 97, 100, 102, 106) sts.
Row 10: BO 0 (0, 0, 0, 0, 0, 0, 1, 2) sts, P to end. 62 (69, 78, 81, 92, 97, 100, 101, 104) sts.
Work 30 (32, 36, 36, 38, 42, 46, 50, 54) rows in St st.

Shape Back Neck
Row 1 (RS): K21 (23, 25, 26, 29, 31, 33, 35, 35) sts for Right Shoulder, BO 20 (23, 28, 29, 34, 35, 34, 31, 34) sts, K to end for Left Shoulder.
Put Right Shoulder sts on a st holder.

Left Shoulder
Row 2 (WS): P.
Row 3: BO 2 (2, 2, 2, 3, 3, 2, 2, 2) sts, K to end. 19 (21, 23, 24, 26, 28, 31, 33, 33) sts.
Row 4: P.
Row 5: BO 1 (2, 1, 1, 1, 1, 1, 1, 1) sts, K to end. 18 (19, 22, 23, 25, 27, 30, 32, 32) sts.
Row 6: P.
Row 7: BO 0 (0, 0, 1, 1, 1, 0, 0, 0) sts, K to end. 18 (19, 22, 22, 24, 26, 30, 32, 32) sts.
Work in St st for 5 (5, 5, 9, 9, 9, 9, 9, 9) rows.
Next Row: BO all sts.

Right Shoulder

Re-join the yarn to work the Right Shoulder with RS facing.

Row 2: K.

Row 3: BO 2 (2, 2, 2, 3, 3, 2, 2, 2) sts, P to end. 19 (21, 23, 24, 26, 28, 31, 33, 33) sts.

Row 4: K.

Row 5: BO 1 (2, 1, 1, 1, 1, 1, 1, 1) sts, P to end. 18 (19, 22, 23, 25, 27, 30, 32, 32) sts.

Row 6: K.

Row 7: BO 0 (0, 0, 1, 1, 1, 0, 0, 0) sts, P to end. 18 (19, 22, 22, 24, 26, 30, 32, 32) sts.

Work in St st for 5 (5, 5, 9, 9, 9, 9, 9, 9) rows.

Next Row: BO all sts.

Front

Re-join the yarn to work the Front, with RS facing.

Row 1 (RS): BO 3 (3, 4, 4, 4, 4, 5, 6, 6) sts, K to end. 73 (84, 94, 101, 112, 123, 129, 135, 142) sts.

Row 2 (WS): BO 3 (3, 4, 4, 4, 4, 5, 6, 6) sts, P to end. 70 (81, 90, 97, 108, 119, 124, 129, 136) sts.

Row 3: BO 2 (3, 3, 3, 3, 4, 5, 6, 6) sts, K to end. 68 (78, 87, 94, 105, 115, 119, 123, 130) sts.

Row 4: BO 2 (3, 3, 3, 3, 4, 5, 6, 6) sts, P to end. 66 (75, 84, 91, 102, 111, 114, 117, 124) sts.

Row 5: BO 1 (2, 2, 3, 3, 4, 4, 5, 5) sts, K to end. 65 (73, 82, 88, 99, 107, 110, 112, 119) sts.

Row 6: BO 1 (2, 2, 3, 3, 4, 4, 5, 5) sts, P to end. 64 (71, 80, 85, 96, 103, 106, 107, 114) sts.

Row 7: BO 1 (1, 1, 2, 2, 3, 3, 2, 3) sts, K to end. 63 (70, 79, 83, 94, 100, 103, 105, 111) sts.

Row 8: BO 1 (1, 1, 2, 2, 3, 3, 2, 3) sts, P to end. 62 (69, 78, 81, 92, 97, 100, 103, 108) sts.

Row 9: BO 0 (0, 0, 0, 0, 0, 0, 1, 2) sts, K to end. 62 (69, 78, 81, 92, 97, 100, 102, 106) sts.

Row 10: BO 0 (0, 0, 0, 0, 0, 0, 1, 2) sts, P to end. 62 (69, 78, 81, 92, 97, 100, 101, 104) sts.

Work 22 (24, 28, 28, 30, 34, 38, 42, 46) rows in St st.

Shape Front Neck

Row 1 (RS): K21 (24, 28, 29, 32, 34, 37, 38, 39) sts for Left Shoulder, BO 20 (21, 22, 23, 28, 29, 26, 25, 26) sts, K to end for Right Shoulder.

Put Left Shoulder sts on st holder and work Right Shoulder.

Right Shoulder

Row 2 (WS): P.

Row 3: BO 2 (2, 2, 3, 3, 3, 3, 3, 3) sts, K to end. 19 (22, 26, 26, 29, 31, 34, 35, 36) sts.

Row 4: P.

Row 5: BO 1 (2, 2, 2, 2, 2, 2, 2, 2) sts, K to end. 18 (20, 24, 24, 27, 29, 32, 33, 34) sts.

Row 6: P.

Row 7: BO 0 (1, 1, 1, 2, 2, 1, 1, 2) sts, K to end. 18 (19, 23, 23, 25, 27, 31, 32, 32) sts.

Row 8: P.

Row 9: BO 0 (0, 1, 1, 1, 1, 1, 0, 0) sts, K to end. 18 (19, 22, 22, 24, 26, 30, 32, 32) sts.

Work in St st for 11 (11, 11, 15, 15, 15, 15, 15, 15) rows.

Next Row: BO all sts.

Left Shoulder

Re-join the yarn to work the Left Shoulder sts with RS facing.

Row 2 (RS): K.

Row 3 (WS): BO 2 (2, 2, 3, 3, 3, 3, 3, 3) sts, P to end. 19 (22, 26, 26, 29, 31, 34, 35, 36) sts.

Row 4: K.

Row 5: BO 1 (2, 2, 2, 2, 2, 2, 2, 2) sts, P to end. 18 (20, 24, 24, 27, 29, 32, 33, 34) sts.

Row 6: K.

Row 7: BO 0 (1, 1, 1, 2, 2, 1, 1, 2) sts, P to end. 18 (19, 23, 23, 25, 27, 31, 32, 32) sts.

Row 8: K.

Row 9: BO 0 (0, 1, 1, 1, 1, 1, 0, 0) sts, P to end. 18 (19, 22, 22, 24, 26, 30, 32, 32) sts.

Work in St st for 11 (11, 11, 15, 15, 15, 15, 15, 15) rows.

Next Row: BO all sts.

Finishing

Weave in ends, wash and block to diagram.
Sew shoulder seams together.

Neckband

PU & K 148 (150, 154, 158, 162, 166, 170, 174, 178) sts around the neck. PM for beginning of rnd. Work 8 rnds in Seed st. BO all sts.

LH Milanese Lace Panel

8	7	6	5	4	3	2	1	
					O	λ		10
				O		λ		9
			O			λ		8
		O				λ		7
λ	O							6
	λ					O		5
		λ				O		4
			λ			O		3
				λ		O		2
					λ	O		1

RH Milanese Lace Panel

8	7	6	5	4	3	2	1	
	/	O						10
	/		O					9
	/			O				8
	/				O			7
						O	/	6
	O				/			5
	O			/				4
	O		/					3
	O	/						2
	O	/						1

Legend

☐	**knit**
O	**yo** — Yarn Over
/	**k2tog** — Knit two stitches together as one stitch
λ	**sl1 k psso** — slip one, knit one, pass slipped stitch over, knit one
☐	**Pattern Repeat**

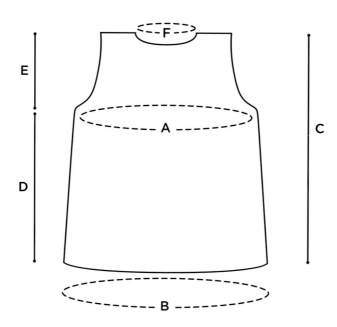

A 34 (38.25, 42.25, 46.25, 50.25, 54.25, 58.25, 62.5, 66.5)"
B 36.25 (40.5, 44.5, 48.5, 52.5, 56.5, 60.5, 64.5, 68.6)"
C 24.5 (24.75, 25.25, 25.75, 26.25, 26, 26.5, 27.25, 27.75)"
D 17 (17, 17, 17, 17, 16.25, 16.25, 16.25, 16.25)"
E 7.5 (7.75, 8.25, 8.75, 9.25, 9.75, 10.25, 11, 11.5)"
F 27 (27.25, 28, 28.75, 29.5, 30, 31, 31.5, 32.25)"

ZIG SWEATER

by Violet LeBeaux

FINISHED MEASUREMENTS

32 (36, 40, 44, 48, 52)" finished waist measurement

YARN

Knit Picks Palette
(100% Peruvian Highland Wool; 231 yards/50g): MC Blush 23718, 4 (4, 5, 5, 6, 6) balls; C1 Cream 23730, 2 (2, 2, 2, 3, 3) balls

NEEDLES

US 6 (4mm) circular needles, or size to obtain gauge
US 6 (4mm) DPN or two 24" circular needles for two circulars technique, or one 32" or longer circular needle for Magic Loop technique, or size to obtain gauge

NOTIONS

Yarn Needle
Stitch Markers
Stitch holder or scrap yarn

GAUGE

22 sts and 32 rnds = 4" over St st in the rnd, blocked
20 sts and 28 rows = 4" over Zigzag Lace, blocked

Notes:

Zig is a summer-friendly boat neck, cropped sleeve sweater featuring simple lace on the shoulders and arms. The design is flattering and wearable while being a basic construction easy enough for beginners to understand and customize. The light fabric makes it perfect for warmer weather.

Zig is constructed bottom up beginning in the round and then switches to flat at the arm holes. The lace is an easy to memorize zigzag which meets at the top of the shoulders. With stockinette forming the main sections, this is a great first sweater project.

Right Zigzag Stitch Pattern (worked flat over multiples of 2 sts)
Row 1 (RS): (YO, K2tog) to end.
Row 2 (WS): (P2tog, YO) to end.
Rep Rows 1-2 for pattern.

Left Zigzag Stitch Pattern (worked flat over multiples of 2 sts)
Row 1 (RS): (SSK, YO) to end.
Row 2 (WS): (YO, SSP) to end.
Rep Rows 1-2 for pattern

If using the charts, read the chart RS rows (odd numbers) from right to left, and WS rows (even numbers) from left to right.

Lifted Increases
Left Lifted Increase (LLI): K 1 into the st below the previously worked st on the right needle.
Right Lifted Increase (RLI): K 1 into the st below the next st on left needle.

DIRECTIONS

Body
The body section is worked bottom-up in the rnd.

Hem Band and Set Up
With C1, loosely CO 176 (198, 220, 242, 264, 286) sts, PM and join to work in the rnd being careful not to twist.
Rnd 1: K 88 (99, 110, 121, 132, 143), PM, K to end.
Work 23 rnds in St st.
Note: This section will be folded in half and stitched down to form the bottom band during finishing.
Switch to MC and work in St st until MC section measures 1.5 (1.5, 1.75, 2, 2.5, 3)".

Increases
This section increases the st count to make the batwing shape up to the bottom of the cuffs.
Rnd 1: K1, LLI, K to 1 st before M, RLI, K1, SM, K1, LLI, K to last st, RLI, K1. 4sts inc.
Rnds 2-3: K to end.
Repeat Rnds 1-3 a further 43 times. Work measures approximately 21 (21, 21.25, 21.5, 22, 22.5)" from the CO edge. 352 (374, 396, 418, 440, 462) sts.
Place half of the sts on a holder and move on to Upper Body section. 176 (187, 198, 209, 220, 231) sts.

Upper Body
Upper Body/Sleeve
This section is worked flat with MC.

Work in St st until section measures approximately 2.5 (3, 3.25, 3.5, 4, 4)".

Next Row (RS): K 56 (58, 62, 66, 70, 72) sts for sleeve, BO 64 (71, 74, 77, 80, 87) sts for chest, K to the end for second sleeve. Place sleeve sts on hold.

Zigzag Lace Right Side
This section is worked flat with C1. Place the 56 (58, 62, 66, 70, 72) sts for the sleeve on the right side of the work when facing back on needle.
Place sleeve sts back on needle, ready to work a RS row.
Row 1 (RS): K1, work Row 1 of Right Zigzag Stitch Pattern until last st, K1.
Row 2 (WS): P1, work Row 2 of Right Zigzag Stitch Pattern until last st, P1.
Repeat Rows 1-2 until section measures approximately 1.5", ending with Row 2.
Move on to the Zigzag Lace Left Side section with the other sleeve sts.

Zigzag Lace Left Side
This section is worked flat with C1 using the 56 (58, 62, 66, 70, 72) sts for the sleeve on the left side of the work when facing. Place sleeve sts back on needle, ready to work a RS row.
Row 1 (RS): K1, work Row 1 of Left Zigzag Stitch Pattern until last st, K1.
Row 2 (WS): P1, work Row 2 of Left Zigzag Stitch Pattern until last st, P1.
Repeat Rows 1-2 until section measures approximately 1.5", ending with Row 2.

Repeat Upper Body/Sleeve section and Zigzag Lace Right and Left Side sections using remaining 176 (187, 198, 209, 220, 231) sts.
Graft the Zigzag sections together using a 3 needle BO or BO all sts and sew along the shoulder seam to finish the sleeves. Move on to Collar and Cuffs section.

Collar and Cuffs
Collar
This section is worked in the round with C1.
Starting in the back left corner, PU & K 14 Left Zigzag sts, PU & K 66 (71, 74, 76, 82, 86) chest sts, PU & K14 Right Zigzag sts, and PU & K 66 (71, 74, 76, 82, 86) back sts. PM and join to work in the rnd. 160 (170, 176, 180, 192, 200) sts.

Rnd 1: K to end.
Rnd 2: *K30 (15, 20, 28, 10, 8), K2tog; rep from * to end. 155 (160, 168, 174, 176, 180) sts.
Work in St st until section measures approximately 3".
BO all sts.

Cuffs
This section is worked in the round with C1.
PU 44 (50, 52, 55, 61, 61) sts along sleeve edge.
Work in St st for 24 rnds.
BO all sts. Repeat for other sleeve.

Finishing
Fold the Hem Band section in half and sew the edge down. Repeat this with the Collar and Cuffs. Weave in ends, wash and block to diagram.

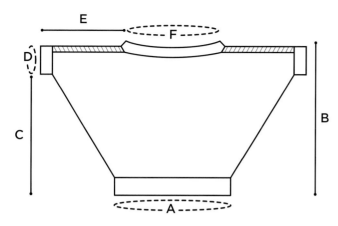

A 32 (36, 40, 44, 48, 52)"
B 25 (25.5, 26, 26.5, 27.5, 28)"
C 19.5 (19.5, 19.75, 20, 20.5, 21)"
D 8 (9, 9.5, 10, 11, 11)"
E 13 (13.5, 14, 15, 15.5, 16)"
F 28.25 (29, 30.5, 31.75, 32, 32.75)"

Left Zigzag Stitch Chart

Right Zigzag Stitch Chart

Legend

yo
Yarn Over

ssk
RS: Slip one stitch as if to knit. Slip another stitch as if to knit. Insert left-hand needle into front of these two stitches and knit them together.
WS: Slip one stitch as if to knit, slip another stitch as if to knit. Slip these two stitches back to left needle in new orientation. Purl them together through the back loop.

k2tog
RS: Knit two stitches together as one stitch
WS: Purl two stitches together as one stitch

Abbreviations

BO	bind off
BOR	beginning of round
cn	cable needle
CC	contrast color
CDD	Centered double dec
CO	cast on
cont	continue
dec	decrease(es)
DPN(s)	double pointed needle(s)
EOR	every other row
inc	increase
K	knit
K2tog	knit two sts together
KFB	knit into the front and back of stitch
K-wise	knitwise
LH	left hand
M	marker
M1	make one stitch
M1L	make one left-leaning stitch
M1R	make one right-leaning stitch
MC	main color
P	purl
P2tog	purl 2 sts together
PM	place marker
PFB	purl into the front and back of stitch
PSSO	pass slipped stitch over
PU	pick up
P-wise	purlwise
rep	repeat
Rev St st	reverse stockinette stitch
RH	right hand
rnd(s)	round(s)
RS	right side
Sk	skip
Sk2p	sl 1, k2tog, pass slipped stitch over k2tog: 2 sts dec
SKP	sl, k, psso: 1 st dec
SL	slip
SM	slip marker
SSK	sl, sl, k these 2 sts tog
SSP	sl, sl, p these 2 sts tog tbl
SSSK	sl, sl, sl, k these 3 sts tog
St st	stockinette stitch
sts	stitch(es)
TBL	through back loop
TFL	through front loop
tog	together
W&T	wrap & turn (see specific instructions in pattern)
WE	work even
WS	wrong side
WYIB	with yarn in back
WYIF	with yarn in front
YO	yarn over

Knit Picks yarn is both luxe and affordable—a seeming contradiction trounced! But it's not just about the pretty colors; we also care deeply about fiber quality and fair labor practices, leaving you with a gorgeously reliable product you'll turn to time and time again.

THIS COLLECTION FEATURES

Comfy Sport
Sport Weight

75% Pima Cotton, 25% Acrylic

CotLin
DK Weight

70% Tangius Cotton, 30% Linen

Shine
Worsted and Sport Weights

60% Pima Cotton,
40% Modal® natural beech wood fiber

Palette
Fingering Weight

100% Peruvian Highland Wool

Lindy Chain
Fingering Weight

70% Linen, 30% Pima Cotton

Curio
Lace Weight

100% Cotton

View these beautiful yarns and more at www.Knit Picks.com